To Cent

Best Wishes!

Craig McCarty

RINKSIDE

RINKSIDE

*A Family's Story
of Courage & Inspiration*

CRAIG McCARTY

BENCHMARK PRESS

A Division of Triumph Books

CHICAGO

© 1998 Craig McCarty and Triumph Books. All rights reserved.

No part of this publication may be reproduced, stored in a retrieval system, or transmitted, in any form by any means, electronic, mechanical, photocopying, or otherwise, without the prior written permission of the publisher, Triumph Books, 601 South LaSalle Street, Suite 500, Chicago, Illinois 60605.

This book is available in quantity at special discounts for your group or organization. For more information, contact:

Benchmark Press
A Division of Triumph Books
601 South LaSalle Street
Suite 500
Chicago, IL 60605
(312) 939-3330
(312) 663-3557 FAX

Book design by Sue Knopf
Cover design by Salvatore Concialdi

ISBN 1-892049-09-0

Printed in the United States of America

Photographs courtesy of the McCarty family, except for the photographs found on the following pages: 2, 119, 123, 134, 171, 173, 180, and 198, which are by Mark Hicks, Detroit Red Wings photographer.

CONTENTS

I would like to dedicate this book to my father-in-law in his memory. His name was Robert Pritchard and he was an influence to both Darren and me. He taught me that you can have dignity even though your body is ravaged with cancer. He also filled in for me when I was unable to be the father Darren needed because of work.

FOREWORD

I played seventeen years of professional baseball with the Detroit Tigers and Los Angeles Dodgers. Throughout those years I learned many lessons. The biggest—never stop listening and learning.

Darren and Craig McCarty have two Stanley Cups to celebrate, just as my Dad and I have two World Series Trophies on our mantles. Sounds like just a couple of fathers and sons who were lucky and realized their dreams. Realized our dreams, yes. Lucky, I'm not sure.

Have you ever been told the harder you work, the luckier you get? Are you willing to pay the price? It's not about what you *are doing* as much as what you're *not doing*. These are things that both Darren and I were told, **by our parents!**

Now, as the parent of children partcipating in sports, my role seems to be reversed. Do I have a dream of watching my young son hoist the Cup? Would I like my son to hit the game-winning home run? Of course! But is that really what life is all about? No, that is only the end result. It's about family. Being the *best family* you can be through all the trials and tribulations that will be thrown at you along the way.

Craig McCarty sees life much like I do. Realizing that each day is a gift and that love and support from family are the ingredients that sustain and nourish both parents and children alike!

Kirk Gibson

Introduction

Darren and Craig at the Foundation's first gala fundraising event.

My son, Darren, started the McCarty Cancer Foundation on Father's Day 1997. He felt that, with his presence in the Detroit market as a hockey player and a personality, we could make a difference in the lives of people living with multiple myeloma (the kind of cancer I have). We both felt that we could be an example to others and, hopefully, allow them the opportunity of learning from our experience. Writing a book about the McCarty Cancer Foundation was not the first thing that came to my mind when Darren started it, but when I did come up with the idea, it seemed like another way to help others.

Cancer is a disease that is bigger than both Darren and me. Alcoholism is also a disease that is bigger than both Darren and me. Unfortunately, I have cancer. And unfortunately, Darren is an alcoholic. We decided to deal with our diseases together, no matter what the outcome, to be there for each other.

We both realize that our story is not different from the stories of most people who are reading this book. Many people have problems far greater than ours. We are appreciative that our problems are not as great as others and that we lead fairly normal lives.

This is not a story about a famous hockey player but a story about real family life and some of the things we have done to overcome our shortcomings. The final outcome for Darren and me is still to be determined. Each day has its own stresses and strains. I hope you will learn from both our success and our mistakes, and we will help you realize that dealing with your problems can make you stronger.

One thing that Darren is always reminded of is my request that he has a plan. From the time he was very young, he wanted to play sports. I kept telling him, "you have to pay the price to succeed and have a plan." I am glad he listened because his plan was to do exactly what he is doing. I am learning from him what commitment is.

I hope, through the following chapters, to give you insight into how our family has coped with the challenges presented to us. And I hope this helps you successfully cope with your own challenges.

The Beginning

From an early age,
Darren's goal was to play
in the NHL.
He did not waver from this goal
from the age of five.

Many people look to Darren as a star hockey player. It is difficult for me as a parent to separate the life of Darren McCarty, hockey player for the Detroit Red Wings, and of Darren McCarty, my son. I am still in awe when I see Darren on the ice and, especially, when I saw him with the Stanley Cup.

I played hockey as a young Canadian boy. All the games, whether they were on the ice, in a basement, or on the road, were played for the Stanley Cup. Back then, there were not the teams in the National Hockey League that there are now. The teams got some press, but not like they do today. The game has become international, with players from all over the world competing for a job.

From an early age, Darren's goal was to play in the NHL. He did not waver from this goal from the age of five. It was a challenge for us as a family to accept Darren and his goals. When he was young, it was cute when he told people he wanted to be a professional hockey player. But when he was in his early teens and still told his teachers that he wanted to be a professional hockey player, it became embarrassing.

Growing up, I lacked goals and an understanding about the commitment it takes to make dreams come true. Over the years, I took many courses in life, and I learned that you have to set a goal and stay with it if it is truly what you want.

The First Season

Darren was not always the best player when he was young. The first year he played hockey he didn't like wearing the garter belt to hold the socks in place. We had such a fight about it that the equipment went into the closet and no hockey was played the first year. He was five years old.

So Many Sports, So Little Time

The next year when Darren asked to play hockey, my wife, Roberta, and I reminded him of the problems we had the year before. He promised us we would have no problems this time and that he would do whatever he had to do to play. It turned out to be a lot of fun for the family. The kids at this age played on only part of the ice, and it was fun to watch them skate around, fall down, and get back up again.

Darren played on what we called a house league team. These teams are picked from the kids in the same age group and are put together so they can compete with each other on an even scale. They have

Craig and Darren, already an aspiring hockey player at age five, on the ice.

practice once a week and usually one game a week. The games are competitive and most of the kids are at the same level of play. Darren was never a good skater, but he was determined and it showed.

During the first couple of years of house league we were approached by travel league coaches who felt Darren should be playing travel hockey. They said he was wasting his time playing house league and that he would get better by playing against better players. We were not sure what to do. As a parent you want your children to succeed, but travel hockey brings a lot of stress on both the family and the player. We were concerned the fun would be taken out if too much pressure was placed on winning.

And the problem was not only in hockey. Darren also played baseball. He was competitive in all aspects of sports. When he was six, we started going from baseball to hockey. It was a never-ending drive from arena to arena or ball diamond to ball diamond. I didn't always handle the commitment we were making well and many "family discussions" were had.

To say Darren had an abundance of energy would be an understatement. He had so much energy that it became a problem in baseball. The first ball team I remember was coached by Max Raffoul. I was working a lot at the time, and I would only get to the games occasionally. I think the first year I made it to only a

As a young boy, Darren frequently divided his time between the base-ball diamond and the hockey arena.

couple of games. The coach approached me once and said he had a problem with Darren.

Darren, it seems, had the idea that he had to be in every play. If they put Darren in right field and a ball was hit to left, Darren would try to make the play. To make him stay in one spot, Max recommended that Darren play catcher on a full-time basis.

Darren was now in on almost every play, and it gave the other kids on the team a chance to field the ball. He still tried to get most pop flies hit into the infield, but over the next few years, he got better at staying in the proper spot. Baseball also brought people who wanted Darren to play travel. But we still were not prepared for the commitment for travel baseball or, for that matter, travel hockey.

The Decision to Travel

The time spent waiting for ball games and hockey games to get started gives you a chance to talk to other parents. Some of the people we talked with had bad experiences with travel sports. They felt there was too much pressure put on the kids to win. Also, some of the coaches would coach only if their kid played in the key positions and a majority of the time.

On the other side, we met many people who felt that travel sports were a great family activity. In fact, we are still friends with many of these people. They have a good family basis and understand that the games are just games and not a life-and-death issue. These people also became close with our kids over the years.

We learned from our friends that the pressure to succeed is good for kids when it is structured and when the effort to play hard is rewarded. A lot of parents pay their kids for goals in hockey. While it was an incentive, we paid Darren more for the assists than the goals. We didn't pay much. I think it was twenty-five cents for a goal and fifty cents for an assist. The idea was lost after the first few years. We knew of parents who paid up to five dollars for a goal. Their kids became puck hogs. They wouldn't pass the puck. Team play was being taken away from them.

Darren was a prolific goal scorer. They were never pretty end-to-end rushes. More often, it was a scramble in front of the net with the puck being pushed in by Darren. He seemed to thrive on the pressure of the game. The more pressure or the more important the game, the more he wanted to play.

Around Christmas of the second year, he was playing house league. I was in the dressing room after a game, which the kids had lost. The mood was solemn, but Darren was in good spirits when a fellow teammate came over to him. The teammate was crying about the loss. Apparently, the boy's father told him the reason they lost was that Darren had not scored enough goals. This kind of unfair remark made me start to see the pressure put on the kids.

The pressure was not from the kids—as a rule, it was from the parents. I found that many of the parents had unrealistic ideas of their kid's talent. Darren was never the most talented player on the team. But he was, and I guess still is, one of the most determined players in whatever he was playing. After a few more incidents with people's kids telling Darren he didn't play well enough to win, we decided maybe travel hockey would be easier.

On the Road

Our first contact with travel sports was in early January on a cold Saturday morning. We met at our local arena to carpool to Sarnia for a couple of games that day.

The morning was cool. We were introduced to some of the other parents, and we started on our journey. The drive was expected to take two hours. Within the first hour, road conditions became slippery, but the sun and the clear sky didn't give the drivers an indication of how slippery it was.

Cars were sliding off the road and spinning in front of us. After two hours of terrible driving we were only halfway there. The coach stopped and called the arena but was informed the game would be played as soon

Darren (third from the left, second row) and his teammates on the Leamington Travel Hockey Team.

as we could get there. The parents driving did a good job of keeping their cars on the road. This was a real indoctrination for the McCarty family to travel hockey. After four hours of terrible driving, we arrived at the arena.

As the kids unloaded the cars and the parents relived the tales of the trip, the coach of one of the teams we were to play came over. He was happy everyone was safe, but our game was cancelled because he couldn't get enough players to ice a team. He said the roads were too dangerous, and he cancelled the game shortly after our phone call. But there was another team who had come the same distance, so we ended up having a game against them. This was just the beginning of travel sports.

The coach for Darren's first travel team explained to us that Darren would play but not as much as he had in house league. He explained that, because there were many good players on the team and winning was important, the best players played the most. It was good for Darren to spend some time watching the games. And he had a great deal of enthusiasm, which he used to cheer on his team.

I am glad Darren is able to channel his enthusiasm to the sport. Darren, to this day, is the same person he was when he was six years old. When someone scores, he is happy for them and for the team. He has a determined attitude about winning. But it is not a win-at-all-costs attitude.

Travel Sports

*Our lives revolved
around Darren
and his sports.
It seemed that every night
we had someplace to go
for a game or practice.*

The years that followed were difficult for me to deal with. It is a great commitment to be a parent of a travel sport player. There is the time spent driving from ball diamond to ball diamond or arena to arena, plus the practices, equipment costs, and travel expenses. Darren was always breaking equipment, whether it was in hockey or baseball. For the next five to seven years there was a lot of arguing about how much time was spent playing sports.

Darren also played soccer and basketball at school. There were times when he would change in the car from one sport to another. Our lives revolved around Darren and his sports. I would get upset about the time required and the financial commitment. It seemed that every night we had someplace to go for a game or practice.

Roberta and I got into some pretty ugly arguments about the commitment. She had grown up in a family where sports were played and the commitment was second nature. My family background was not the same. I wanted to play, but we couldn't afford the expense. As an adult, I was under the opinion that it was a waste of money because most of the kids that played were playing only because their parents wanted them to.

Overbearing Parents

I was continually shocked at how some parents treated their kids. If the kid had a bad game, the parent would belittle the kid on the ride home. It was over the next few years that these kids started to drop out of sports. I know some of these kids wanted to play, but their parents made it so bad they ended up quitting.

I figured that, as long as Darren was going to play, I might as well get involved. I first helped by coaching one of Darren's ball teams. Through that head coach and my own experiences, I found out it was mostly the parents who caused the kids to act up.

In the spring, the kids would have tryouts for the ball team. This is a difficult time for the parents, the kids, and the coaches. The kids just want to play, and they usually understand if they do not make the team. In this process, you pick the kids whose parents will allow you to coach.

As a first-time coach, I learned about the parents who thought they could just tell us to take their son or daughter. (This was about the time that girls were starting to play boys' baseball also.) Coaching the kids was one thing, but dealing with a parent who had other ideas of how the team should work was quite another. There was one boy who was good, but his father was completely out of control. In team sports, as we were learning, the chemistry of the players is more important than the skill. Unfortunately, we chose to keep the boy on the team. This was against the judgement of the head coach and because of my pleading. After this, I learned to listen to others who had coached before.

The major problem was that the boy was coached by his father during the games. He would look to the third-base coach for the batting signals and then turn around and look at his father for signals. Not only did it delay the game, but it also made it impossible to keep the team morale up. This father also had a running commentary going during the game to educate the parents about how the game should be coached.

After the first month the head coach came to me and said we were going to have to cut the player because the disruption was more then he could deal with. Apparently this was not the first time the boy had been cut because of his father. The father was very upset, but I know the boy understood what a disruption his dad was. I learned that when you trust a coach to coach, you leave the kids alone and don't second-guess.

Over the next twenty years when I had the urge to talk to a coach about the sport Darren was playing, I remembered that lesson and kept my mouth shut. The

Baseball taught Darren that in sports, teamwork means more than individual talent.

other lesson Roberta and I learned was to not get too caught up in the emotion of the game. This was not a lesson I learned immediately but over a period of a couple of years. I would yell at the referees in hockey and the umpires in baseball. It took me some time to realize what a fool I was making of myself and that all my yelling didn't change the outcome of the game.

It's All About Teamwork

The games were exciting and I would get caught up with the plays. The skill level of the kids was not always the same, so every once in a while you would be in a blowout game. Sometimes it was for you, and other times against you. The good coaches taught the kids not to worry about a loss and they kept the highs of the victory in line.

One of the ball teams Darren played on was going for the Provincial Championship played on Labor Day as a tournament. The top teams from each region would play double elimination. In other words, you had to lose two games to be eliminated. Our boys won all their games until we met one team who could hit and field better than we had seen all season.

The kids were intimidated by the other team. The game was played with our best players, and we got our butts whipped in game one. The coach of the other team came up to me and the other coach with a deal.

He told us we were totally outclassed and he would play his second-string kids to make the next game closer. He said he would also understand if we wanted to forfeit the game so as not to embarrass our players.

We had a meeting with the kids. We had no intention of forfeiting the game. We told the kids we thought they could beat this team if they decided to play together as a team. And as it turned out, we won games two and three. The other team had been so sure about victory that they had not made arrangements for overnight accommodations. They ended up driving thirty miles for hotel rooms only to come back on Sunday and have us beat them. It meant the final game would be on Monday, and again, they had to find rooms. Some of them slept in their cars at the ballpark.

The next game wasn't even close. We had kids making diving catches and hitting the ball better than ever. Teamwork does win over individual talent. This was a lesson that both Darren and I learned time and time again. The victory game was followed by a party and a ride through town on a fire engine. This was the first victory celebration for the McCarty family.

An Extended Family

It was in these early years of baseball and hockey that we decided to make sports a family affair. Melissa was born and attended her first hockey game at the tender age of three weeks. Over the next fifteen years, she attended all the hockey and ball games with us. She got to meet many great people and associate with the brothers and sisters of the other team players.

We have, over the years, still kept in contact with many of these people and keep them in our close circle of friends. They were the people who helped when I was sick and gave words of encouragement to my wife and family when things were not going well. We watch with pleasure at the kinds of adults these kids have become. I have watched as they have gone on to get married and raise kids of their own. I am happy to say that most of them have turned into productive adults who understand they have to give back to the community.

One of Darren's biggest pleasures is a baseball bat given to him by his old ball teammates Jason Wuerch and Piero Ingratta. Jason had used the bat when he played professional baseball in the New York Yankees organization. The bat was autographed by the entire team which Jason and Piero coached.

The best part about the travel is the relaxation after the game with the other parents. We were warned to be on the lookout for troublemakers and, above all, not to open our hotel room door if an urgent knock came. The first road game with an overnight stay was near Toronto, and true to form, it was an adventure. We checked in and were assigned a room near the rest of the team. As luck would have it, at about two in the morning there was an urgent knock on our door. Remembering what I had been warned, I looked out the peephole to see a couple of the fathers drunk as skunks. They had a bucket of water and intended to douse the person who opened the door. I didn't open the door and, instead, talked them into leaving and going back to their own rooms.

Many of the parents were resourceful when it came to traveling. They would travel with electric fry pans, portable ovens, and more food than we could ever eat. There was never a shortage of food to munch on or discussions about the games. At first we tried to second guess the coaches' decisions. As time passed we learned it is better to let the coaches have the kids with little interference from the parents. I learned this lesson from the ballpark.

This did not happen overnight. It took a couple of years for us to see who felt as we did. It seemed that the people who complained the most where the parents who had the greatest expectations for their children. There are exceptions to all rules and this was no different. We did see a gradual change over the next four to five years of players coming and leaving the teams. In most instances, if a boy left, he was leaving because his parents had made it difficult for the coaching staff to coach him.

We must always remember that hockey and baseball are sports and games. The importance for these kids when they are young is to learn how to lose as well as how to win. Baseball was a sport that Darren excelled in, but hockey was his true love. When he was about seven he started to come out with my Sunday morning hockey team. He took any chance he could to play hockey, whether it was ice hockey or road hockey.

Dangerous Driving

Darren, from the time he started playing hockey, was always different. After the first year of hockey, he wouldn't let anyone help him with his equipment. Sometimes on the ice his pants would fall down, so he started to tie them up with a skate lace—something he still does to this day. There were times I would look out and see that his skates were not tight enough, but I knew he wouldn't want me to touch them.

Driving in the summer for baseball was easy compared to driving for hockey. The winters created many driving adventures as well as many tense moments. One time after a late night, I told Darren he had to talk to keep me awake during the drive home. He talked the entire three hours, and to this day we still remember that night with fondness.

One Easter weekend we left a spot near Toronto to drive home to be with the family for my grandmother's eighty-fifth birthday. The road was clear for a while, but then the snow started. It was horrible. The main roads were closed and the side roads were black ice. What usually was a four-hour trip turned into an eight-hour marathon. There was an intense blizzard for seventy miles and then nothing. When we got home and told people, they thought we were crazy. The sun was out and the temperature was in the low fifties. Some of the people didn't make it home that night and ended up staying in farm houses along the side roads.

Over the next ten years there were only one or two times when we were stopped from getting home or going to a game. We were always cautious and watched the weather to see what was ahead, but it did make for some tense travel.

Hockey Camp

It was during this time that Darren started to excel in hockey. He seemed to have a knack for being in the right spot to help with an assist or score a goal. There was pressure placed on him by the coaches, and he accepted it. We found ourselves watching with pleasure as he would celebrate a goal with one of his teammates. It wasn't important to him who scored. To this day he still celebrates all the goals, even if he is not involved on the ice.

We also noticed that Darren was being put on the ice in key situations. Sometimes he would help with a win, and other times they would lose. The point is that he learned to deal with the pressures of sports when he was young. This is something that not all kids can handle. I saw many kids who, skill-wise, were much better than Darren, but they couldn't handle the pressure placed on them. I would be lying if I said Darren was the best player on his teams. He was never the best, but he was always the most intense. He had heart for the game; whether it was baseball or hockey. Heart is something you either have or don't. I don't think it can be taught.

Darren did not look pretty when he skated. He had a wide, choppy stance with poor balance. What he lacked in skating, he made up for in enthusiasm. We felt he would improve if he could get some lessons from a professional instructor. After consulting some people and reading many brochures, we decided on a hockey school for Darren. The school was held in August and required him to stay over for a week-long camp. The first year was the hardest on us because we worried about leaving our eight-year-old boy with others. The camp was located in a university town, and the players stayed at the campus. Darren enjoyed this so much he wanted to go back year after year, and over the next eight years, he began to show some true ability to accompany his desire.

*By age eight, Darren was already telling people about his goal to play
in the National Hockey League.*

It was about the time when Darren was eight that he started to tell people he was going to play in the National Hockey League. Darren set up a goal in his mind and never wavered from it.

The Shed

Over the years, Darren worked on his skating and his shooting so much it caused problems. At the back of our lot was a shed used to store the garden tools. It was existing when we bought the house and was made out of thick barn lumber. I won't say it was a good building, but it was a sturdy shed with a door. I was working a lot of hours back then, so I didn't always get a chance to keep up with what was going on around the house. One night I went out to the shed and Darren had painted a picture of a goaltender on the side of the shed using spray paint.

I asked Darren about the picture, and he explained it was a target so he could learn how to score. The goalie he was using was Billy Smith of the New York Islanders. (Years later during an Adirondack Red Wings game, Billy Smith was sitting in front of Roberta and me. I was tempted to tell him about his role in Darren's development and I regret never taking a picture of it.) This was also about the same time I found a steel disc the size of a hockey puck. It was so heavy that I had a difficult time shooting it. Darren spent hours shooting this disc at our shed.

I will tell you that a steel disc the size of a hockey puck can cause some damage. It wasn't long before Darren had shot out the side of the shed. I hope that he has the same patience my wife instructed me to have when his son takes out a window or a garage door! The shed then had to come down because it was unsafe. I then took the puck away from Darren to make sure he didn't start on the house.

Sibling Rivalry

When Melissa was seven, Darren started to use her as a goaltender. He set her in a make-believe goal and shot anything from rolled-up socks to tin foil at her. We learned in later years that she hated this but she did it for her big brother. To this day they still act like brother and sister, which means they fight, argue, and give each other grief. I do know they respect each other, but at times, it doesn't show.

Being the sister of Darren has its challenges. There are times when I am sure Melissa loves the attention, and then there are times when she wishes he was not related. Melissa became, over the years, tired of being referred to as Darren's little sister. She has made it her goal to be a person of her own and not let her brother's stardom cast a shadow on her. When she was in high school, she wrote a story about being Darren McCarty's sister. The story won an award and showed to all that

Melissa McCarty made sure people knew she wasn't just "Darren's little sister."

she would not sit back and just be "Darren's sister." Darren was her brother, but he was also her best friend. If anything, she holds Darren to a higher level of responsibility than the rest of the family.

I Don't Have a Name
by Melissa McCarty

I don't have a name.

Okay, that's a lie. On my birth certificate it reads: Melissa Lea (pronounced Lee) McCarty. But in all actuality, it should read: Darren McCarty's sister (or something to that effect).

Having a brother in the NHL is, to say the least, interesting. I get to attend a lot of games, meet a lot of people, and generally do things I normally wouldn't get to do. But there is a dark side to it as well.

Because your brother is in the NHL, people expect a lot from you. People always ask me if I play hockey and I tell them I don't. When they ask why, I tell them that the reason is because I can't skate. They laugh at me. They always say, "Your brother is in the NHL and you don't even know how to skate?," like it's a law that if your brother plays hockey, you have to as well.

Then comes the fuss of who an NHL player's sister dates. Most guys tell me that they are intimidated by my brother, which really bothers me (because I can beat him up). Or they say how cool it would be to meet him (which gets them an automatic kick to the curb). When I do have a boyfriend, people automatically assume that he's a hockey player. And when he is a hockey player, they say how fitting it is that Darren McCarty's sister is dating a hockey player. When the subject of who I'm going to marry comes up, my grandma is the first one to suggest that I'm going to marry a hockey player. It's funny, though, because when my brother hears that he warns me to stay as far away from hockey players as I can because "they are all trouble." I guess it takes one to know one.

As I'm getting older, I'm trying to decide what I want to be. I've been thinking about getting into sports management, but already people are saying how fitting it is that Darren McCarty's sister wants to have a career in sports. They tell me that I'll have so many opportunities because of my brother. But I also love fashion. I know that the name McCarty won't get me as far in fashion as it will in sports, but it's something I'd like to do. I also like the thought that Donna Karan and Ralph Lauren probably don't care if my brother is in the NHL and have probably never heard of him, or will.

I'm learning to live with the fact that my brother is a celebrity. I just hope that someday I'll be able to make a name for myself and actually get called what I am legally registered as. And who knows, maybe one day someone will say to my brother, "Hey, aren't you the brother of Melissa McCarty, the famous fashion designer?" (A girl can dream, can't she?)

Misbehavin'

Our seasons were planned by the sport de jour. It was either hockey or baseball as travel sport with basketball, soccer, and gymnastics. I was involved in coaching both hockey and baseball. There were many tense times when we were going from sport to sport with no rest in between. We felt that, if the kids were busy with sports, they would have no time to get into trouble.

I remember when Darren was about ten, we went to visit his cousin, Chad. Normally these kids were good, but together they sometimes got carried away. Darren's cousin lived on a farm where they raised chickens for eggs. One time, they threw the eggs against the side of the building. It appeared they were having pitching practice using eggs as baseballs and throwing them against the barn. Hundreds of eggs were lost in the practice. It took the boys quite a while to clean up the mess. They both were punished. We look back on this now and laugh, but I assure you it wasn't funny at the time.

The only other time that Darren got our attention was when he was about thirteen years old. My wife and I were attending a function on a Sunday afternoon so Darren had to watch his sister Melissa. He was told that they had to stay home and that under no circumstances was he to leave our property. He could have other kids over to play baseball in the backyard but he was not to leave.

Roberta and I got home about 6:00 PM to find Darren walking around the house with a toque hat on his head. At first it seemed strange, but we didn't say anything.

Darren, age nine, celebrating Christmas with a new pair of gloves.

It was after we were home about an hour when Melissa spilled the news. In the afternoon, Darren took Melissa to a local church parking lot for a street hockey game. During the game Darren got cut with a stick. They walked to the hospital were the doctor stitched the wound. Darren decided to wear the toque as a way to hide the cut. Of course we were upset that he had disobeyed us. Now when we look back on this we laugh about it, and I am impressed with his maturity to have been able to take care of the problem.

Learning by Example

As a parent you want to protect your kids from the difficulties you faced growing up. We were constantly telling Darren he had to have a dream other than the NHL. He was a good student when he gave school his attention. But school was a time for him to socialize with others he didn't see when he was playing sports.

We encouraged him to work at his school classes so he would have an education if his dream of hockey did not come through. We are happy with the help given to him by many of his teachers and that he succeeded in finishing his high school education.

I have learned that kids have to discover themselves. The environment in which kids grow up is important. I feel fortunate that Darren and Melissa have been around the fine families we associated with when they were young, because there is nothing that teaches like example. I wonder how many times we tell our kids to do one thing and then do the opposite ourselves.

It is difficult to be the parent you want to be. I think we are often a reflection of the people around us. When Darren was playing sports, it became clear to us that his improvement was best when he played with kids equal to or better than him. We were lucky to have a lot of good athletes in the Leamington area for Darren to associate with. He was eager to learn, and we were happy to find families that had the same ideals for their kids.

The coaches Darren had growing up were not necessarily the most skilled in their sport, but they had people skills. Darren was fortunate to have these coaches. They understood he was a competitor who wanted to be in on all the action. When Darren brought the Stanley Cup home, the people he wanted to share it with were the coaches he had growing up. These are the people who toil for years helping kids become adults. They teach lessons about life and team concepts that some kids never learn. We saw many kids over the years who were better than Darren in sports, but they didn't understand the concept of team. And that makes all the difference.

The teams Darren played on usually had a pretty good mix of talent. He was rarely the best player on the team, but he was always trying to improve and practiced many hours. It seemed like a waste of time to me back then, but now I look back and see the dedication he had.

Breaking Them In

When Darren was thirteen, he was breaking sticks at an alarming rate. I went to our local sports shop to discuss the problem. They suggested that Darren was too aggressive, but they were happy to sell us sticks in bulk for the same price as the local junior team was paying. Sticks were not the only problem. The shoulder pads Darren used were new at the beginning of the year, but they were destroyed by Christmas. I went again to the sports shop and ranted and raved about the poor quality of the equipment.

The manager, Jerry Brooks, was a great guy and reminded me that Darren was hard on the equipment. He told me that Darren broke more sticks and equipment than anyone he had ever seen. Jerry also gave me a new set of shoulder pads. I know they couldn't return the old ones in the shape they were in, but he knew how much money we had spent already on equipment. Jerry may not have helped Darren learn to play hockey, but he allowed us, as parents, to keep him playing. We always used his advice on selecting equipment, and truly the sport lost a great person when he died.

By the time he was thirteen, Darren was playing

An avid hockey player by age thirteen, Darren was notorious for breaking his sticks. Here he buys new sticks with travel teammate Steve Young.

hockey every day. His equipment never did dry out. The skates were always wet and weighed about twice what they should have. When Darren got dressed he would tape things and tie things to get them to fit properly. He would tie his pants up with skate laces. His shin pads were usually broken, and his shoulder pads were tied together with skate laces. We would buy new equipment whenever we saw a problem, but he seemed happier once the new things were broken in.

Working Together

At the age of thirteen, Darren was starting to fill out. He was always broad in the shoulders, but he was not among the bigger boys. It was amazing to watch over the years as Darren caught up in size to the others. It was also about this time that some of the smaller kids were being taken advantage of on the ice. Their size and speed were working against them. The bigger kids had gotten the skills to catch up to their body.

It was about this time when Darren decided he wanted to help me with my company and get a summer job. I owned a small heating and air conditioning company that had about twenty-five employees. The work was hot, and the days were long when we were busy. Darren started out with us by cleaning around the shop in the summer. It didn't work out too well the first year. I always told Darren that, as the son of the owner, he had to work harder than the normal employees. I was taught by my grandfather when I worked on the farm that the family had to show the others how hard we had to work. Darren didn't share my views on working hard. He still to this day does not consider hockey as work. It was only in the last couple of years that I began to understand that if you truly enjoy something it isn't work. Darren's goal is to never work outside of hockey. I have learned from him that work does not have to be a struggle. It is up to us to make it a pleasure or not. Once Darren is done with hockey, I hope he finds something that gives him as much pleasure and doesn't consider it "work."

I learned a lesson from Darren during the three years he worked for me. He kept getting fired because I was not going to have him working for me and not working hard. I was hard on him, but the lesson is that if you want something bad enough, you make the sacrifices to get there. Darren wanted not to have to work for me bad enough that he worked extra hard at hockey so it became his job. It was tough for me to view playing hockey as a job, but the more I see the sacrifices the players make, the more I realize how much it is like a normal job.

Over the years, Darren worked hard at making hockey his job.

The Tough Years

Darren always felt the pressure,
but he never let it get to him.
If anything, he seemed to excel
when there was a lot of pressure.
He loved being put into
tight game situations.

The next years proved to be the most problematic for Darren and me as father and son. We were close in the fact that we lived in the same house, but I was becoming much more critical of his desire to play sports. I was concerned he did not fully understand the slim chance he had of making a career out of it.

There was a particular argument that Darren and I had over hockey. I was yelling, as was quite common for me, about his lack of commitment regarding the sport. I wanted him to work out instead of fooling around as I felt he was doing. I remember telling him he wasn't good enough to play professionally and that he should give up any notions about hockey as a career. Later he told me that, because of this argument, he felt he had to prove me wrong. I was wrong in the way I approached the problem, but I am happy for him at the outcome.

Team Players

The instructors at the hockey schools in the summer would give Darren awards for his determination, but the results always came back that his skating was not good enough for him to succeed as a professional. We worked with him on the skating, but he didn't seem to be getting better. By the time he was fourteen, he was skating or playing seven days a week. He was playing bantam with other kids from Leamington and was starting to show some progress.

Darren had a coach who had played college hockey and had a good understanding of the game. This coach helped Darren become a much better player. Mike Klym was a good role model for Darren. With his college experience, Mike was able to show Darren the success which could be reached through hard work and was able to get Darren to understand more about the game. I remember Mike telling Darren that when you have the puck and you have two or three players from the opposing team on you, you pass the puck to your other teammates. It took awhile for him to understand the concept of passing the puck around, but the rewards soon started.

When the kids started to play more of a position game instead of just chasing the puck around, the games started to have some flow. It was amazing to watch the kids develop from individual players to team players. Mike would play the kids fairly evenly until we were in a crunch situation—then he would shorten the bench. The players wanted to win, so they would go along with the strategy. Other teams would play only their best lines against us, and have no "legs" left in the third period of most games. It amazes me today to watch the success of the Detroit Red Wings and how their coach uses the entire bench for most of the game.

We were still not convinced that Darren was making the right decision about sports. After all, what does a fourteen year old know? He would play hockey in the winter and spring with baseball in the summer. Over the next couple of years he improved to the point where people would start to key in on him during games. He always felt the pressure, but he never let it get to him. If anything, he seemed to excel when there was a lot of pressure. He loved being put into tight game situations.

Under Seventeen

At the age of sixteen, Darren went to a series of hockey tryouts for what is called "under seventeen." This is a series of tryouts for boys all under age seventeen, and a team is picked to play against other provinces for an under seventeen tournament. We were fortunate that a family friend, Mike Sadler, was a scout for the Ontario Hockey League. He was in charge of our area. Through Mike we gained a good understanding of what was required for Darren to move on in hockey.

Darren had been cut from the local Junior C team when he was fifteen. It was felt that another year of bantam hockey would make him a better player. His skating was not good enough for him to play Junior and he was told he would have to get a lot better if he wanted to succeed at hockey. That year of bantam he scored more goals than we could even count and it seemed that his play was getting better, but his skating wasn't. That was the summer he went to the try-outs for under seventeen. The first tryout was for the local kids. After the two-day tryout he was informed he would be going to the next tryout in London, Ontario. I will admit I felt Mike was being generous in letting Darren move on. I guess he is a better judge of talent than I was.

The next level was a great test for Darren. He was playing with many kids who were equal to or better than him. I was always amazed that if there was a goal, Darren was usually involved either by scoring or an assist. The reports came back to us that he had some talent but that his skating would not allow him to progress much further. Again, he made the cut, earning a chance to try out for the team in Waterloo. I was still upset about all the time and money spent, but we decided to let him go.

The next tryout proved that he was in over his head. All these kids could skate better and handle the puck with great ease. Darren was a hard worker, but his skating was not up to the standards of other players. I was convinced he would come back home

Darren continued playing baseball after he was cut from the under seventeen team.

and play Junior C hockey if he could make the team. Junior hockey is broken down into levels from Junior A to Junior D. Junior A is the highest level for which you are drafted by teams in the Ontario Hockey League. The better you are, the higher level you are able to play. Many players start out playing at lower levels and move up as their skills improve. The kids playing Junior C hockey were from fifteen to twenty years of age. I felt it was probably going to be a stretch for Darren to play at a level higher than Junior C hockey.

A Lesson in Determination

After he was cut from the under seventeen team, Darren continued playing baseball. He was scheduled to go to the hockey school he had gone to from the time he was eight years old. The school had always been one week with on-ice instruction followed by off-ice games. This year they offered a two-week travel hockey camp. It would be a travel camp to other teams of equal caliber throughout Ontario and Quebec. Darren wanted to try out for this team. It was much more expensive and he would have to be recommended for it. He said he would work to get some of the money and that he would practice extra hard to make the team.

Since I had fired him from working for my company for the past three summers, I informed him he would have to get his own job. He got a job working at McDonald's. He thought this was great. He got to work at his favorite place to eat. The best part of the job was cleanup after closing. If you got to clean up, you also got to eat, at no charge, anything that was left. We would pick him up after he was done at 1:30 in the morning. He also worked at another restaurant and worked out almost every day.

Darren was one of the first kids to have roller blades in our area. He would rollerblade from home to the dock and back, which is five miles. This was just the first sign I saw of his determination.

The hockey school was in August, and he was lucky that a local person would be the coach. Kirk Bowman had played in the NHL for a couple of years and spent many years in Europe. He was a skilled player who would have had a long career in the today's NHL. He coached for years at the hockey school Darren had attended, but this was the first time Darren and Kirk had been together. Kirk was the coach, and the assistant coach was a fellow from Peterborough, Ontario, named Brian Drumm.

The team was playing in a city about a one-and-a-half hour drive from Leamington, and Roberta, Melissa, and I drove over to watch a game. The team had players with all skill levels. Some of the kids had not played much organized hockey. It became apparent that the team was going to have problems winning many games. They were on a trip to play in six cities against summer league teams. These teams would have played together for at least two months. Darren's team had only a couple of practices together.

The game was against the local Junior B team. Some of these kids had a great deal of talent and had played together a lot. The game was very one-sided for the home team. I noticed that Darren seemed to take charge of the players on his team. It was no surprise that Darren was named the captain of the team. He was one of the younger players, but seemed to have the respect of the others. This was a trend which we had seen on other teams, but it became more evident to us through this team. They lost all of the games on the trip, but the team seemed to jell over the ten days. It was Darren's first taste of going "on the road."

Leaving Home

Through his play at the under-seventeen camp, even though he didn't make the team, Darren got an invitation to one of the best Junior B franchises in Ontario: the Waterloo Siskens. Peter Brill was the general manager, and he felt Darren had a chance to make the team. It was amazing that none of the local teams would give him a chance yet Waterloo would. It makes you wonder what people look for in players.

We remember the training camp well. Darren, I am sure, will always remember the training camp. He roomed with another local player who was being looked at as the number-one pick in the Ontario Hockey League draft the coming spring. Over the year, these two would play against each other. This was Darren's first taste of living away from home for hockey.

We then received a phone call to come and pick Darren up because the team had decided not to sign him. Peter told me that if they kept him, he would not play much, and so it would be unfair for them to keep him. They handled it well, and I am sure they wished later that he would have stayed.

Darren informed us he was going to play for the Junior B team in Peterborough. Brian Drumm was the coach of the team, and he had guaranteed Darren a spot on the team if he wanted to play Junior B hockey.

Darren's mother and I were beside ourselves. It was one thing to play for a team in Waterloo, a two-hour drive, and quite another to play in Peterborough which is a five-hour drive in the best of weather. Likewise, Waterloo had a budget of $100,000 and Peterborough had a budget of $25,000. Waterloo had been the All-Ontario champions the year before while Peterborough hadn't won a game the previous year.

We felt like our little boy would be gone soon, and we had to make a decision in a hurry. Labor Day week-

While playing for the Junior B team in Peterborough, Darren formed a close friendship with his coach, Brian Drumm.

end was the training camp, but Brian wanted to meet us and sign Darren up before the camp started. We decided to drive the five hours to Peterborough and meet with Brian.

We went on a Saturday in August. This was the week before Labor Day and the holiday traffic was terrible. We met with Brian at the local Holiday Inn. To this day, Melissa will tell people about Brian asking her if she played hockey. With her hair cut short, he had mistaken her for a boy. She won't let Brian forget his mistake.

Brian had a varied experience in hockey with playing stints in the minors. He had been hired to coach the local Junior B team. As the city had a successful Junior A franchise, I am sure he was thinking of possibly coaching at a higher level in the future. He informed me that Darren could play on the team, and the team would pick up his school costs and living costs.

This was a complicated situation for our family. We had always been close, and it meant Darren would be living away from home with strangers. We had hoped he would be good enough to get a scholarship to a school in the States. We knew little about the Junior B team or the people coaching it. We asked our friend Mike Sadler what he thought we should do. Through conversations with Mike and his contacts in hockey, we came to realize that this was a valuable opportunity for Darren if it was what he really wanted. On a good team like Waterloo he may have not played much. Here, they hadn't won a game in a year so he would have a lot of time to learn how to play.

We drove home from that meeting with a lot running through our minds. Do you let your sixteen year old leave home, or do you make him stay and play at a lower level? We got home and sat down with Darren and Melissa. We felt it was important for everyone to have input. We also felt it was time to let Darren make a decision about his future. We explained the decision was up to him. If he decided to go play hockey, we would support him in it. We didn't want him to come back to us when he was twenty-five and say, "I might have made it to the NHL, but you didn't let me try."

We felt he had a grasp of the situation. We didn't want to be responsible for holding up his dream. We also made a realistic appeal to him to understand the reality of making hockey a career. I remember one of the kids in Darren's Leamington high school telling us about a teacher who told the class that Darren was making a mistake and that he would be back playing hockey in Leamington soon. I guess he underestimated Darren's ability to deal with the amount of work required when you have a dream.

Junior B Hockey

My wife and I watched
as Darren got into a fight
with another player.
This was the first time
we had seen Darren fight;
it was not to be the last.

Junior B marked Darren's transformation into a hockey player. His decision to travel to Peterborough was probably the most important step in his career. Once we made the commitment for him to play, we had a lot of things to get ready. We had to get school marks and find a place to stay. Roberta and I decided that we would try to make as many games as possible. The home games were on Saturday afternoons, which meant we could drive up on Friday night and have the weekend with Darren and see a game.

Darren moved in with his coach Brian Drumm until a home could be found for him to billet. A billet is a family who opens their home to a hockey player. They get paid approximately thirty-five dollars per week to cover room and board. The money they receive barely covers the food, let alone other expenses. The families who billet players truly love the game of hockey and try to make a home environment for players far away from their families. He never did leave Brian's house.

The first tryouts for the team were held in a small arena in Peterborough. Even though Darren was signed to the team, he had to endure the tryout camp. My wife and I watched as Darren got into a fight with another player. This was the first time we had seen Darren fight; it was not to be the last. It didn't last long. Darren hit the other guy in the nose and down he went. His skating was better but still not good enough. He would play on the team and hopefully, with Brian's coaching, he would get better.

The team was terrible for the first two months. They couldn't win a game. As time went on they got a few new players and got better. The season was considered a success when they won a game in November. It even made the front page of the local paper.

A Second Home

We felt strongly about keeping our family together. To this end, we bought a cottage in the area as a home base. Both my wife and I felt it would be our home away from home. Junior B was the beginning of many long road trips, which to this day we would do in a heartbeat. The cottage was just what we needed. It was on a lake, which the kids could play hockey on in the winter or fish in during the spring and fall.

It gave us a chance to keep in touch with Darren and get to know his coach. Brian was just what Darren needed as a coach, a friend, and a disciplinarian. Brian taught Darren how to play position hockey. He taught him when to play hard and when to float. Through his control of the team, Brian was able to control Darren. If Darren missed curfew, we would see him dressed at a game but not playing. After the game we would find out what happened. Darren learned not to miss curfew.

Brian also had a good understanding about what was needed to get drafted into the Ontario Hockey League. There would be games where Darren would get a goal, an assist, and then a fight. This was a Gordie Howe hat trick, according to Brian. It may have impressed Darren, but the rest of the family was not impressed. We felt our son was above these kinds of games. It was our opinion that, if he was good enough, he would be drafted. However, Brian had a better understanding of what the scouts were looking for in a player drafted to the Ontario Hockey League. There was a Junior A team that practiced at the same rink Darren played on. As we watched them practice, it was beyond our comprehension that Darren would ever skate well enough to play Junior A.

Sudden Interest

Brian told us there was a lot of interest in Darren. Other teams had called him regarding the upcoming draft. The Peterborough coaching staff of the Junior A team had made some inquiries about Darren's desire to continue to play Junior hockey or try for a scholarship at a university in the States.

There were also the calls to our house asking what Darren was going to do once his team was out of the league playoffs. Even though they were the last-place team they made the playoffs. The league felt it necessary to extend the season by playing a round-robin type tournament. Each team would have to lose twice to be eliminated. The local Junior B teams had now found out that Darren could play well, so they inquired if Darren would come home early rather than wait to get beat out in Peterborough.

We sat down with Darren and Brian and explained that Darren would probably play more hockey if he came home rather than if he finished the season in Peterborough. We also made it clear that we would support Darren with whatever decision he made. Brian informed us that he had picked up a couple of kids who played some university hockey and that the additions would make the team competitive for the playoffs. Darren had a lot of loyalty to the Peterborough team so he decided to stay in Peterborough.

We also found out that, because the interest in Darren was growing, a good playoff could make a difference as to where he was drafted. Peterborough expressed great interest, but they felt he would not get drafted very high because of his skating. With the draft, the higher you are taken, the better chance you have to make the team. I know the coaches tell everyone they have the same chance when training camp opens, but the people picking the team are usually the same people who scouted the players. It wouldn't look good for the scouts if the high draft picks didn't play well enough to make the team. It is harder for lower draft picks because they come to training camp with a stigma of not being very good because of their draft placing.

We were also told that the Peterborough Junior A team wanted Darren, but they didn't want to take him with a high draft pick. Every player who wants to be drafted has to fill out an application form that indicates the player's preference, either Junior A or going to an American university if offered a scholarship. This is done to let the teams know your intentions.

Peterborough wanted Darren to say he wanted to go to university rather than play Junior A. We discussed this idea and we all agreed it was not the proper thing to do if you wanted to start a new career. We felt Darren deserved the best possible shot at success and starting out with a lie would have been unfair.

The Third Round

When we sent in the form, we received word that Peterborough planned to take Darren in the third round and they felt comfortable it would happen. We thought this was great because our cottage was nearby and life wouldn't have to change. But we quickly learned to expect the unexpected. The draft takes place in arenas around the Junior A hockey system. This draft took place in the North York Arena. The arena starts to fill up at about 9:00 AM. The building is soon full of players with their families as well as a group of agents.

Agents are the blessing and curse of hockey. We have gotten to know some of these people over the past few years and have a great deal of respect for most of them. Unfortunately, some agents prey on kids and their parents. They have a tendency to tell the kids and the parents whatever they want to hear. The reality is that few kids make it from Junior A to the NHL, but some agents paint pictures that are not realistic.

I am not sure what they expect other than to get the kids into their stable. If one of them does make it to the professional ranks, they get a return. In the past, there weren't any requirements to be an agent. Now there is at least a registration requirement for the agents.

We have always felt most kids don't need an agent until just before the NHL draft. One advantage of having an agent and letting others know about it is that it cuts out a lot of wasted time talking to other agents. One of the things we were fortunate to have was a friend who had an agent with a good reputation. He agreed to help us and understood Darren was the person who had the final say. This was a lesson we were to learn in years to come.

The draft is good if you are selected where you want to be and bad if you are one of the kids still sitting there hours later. We were not sure what to expect other than what we were led to believe—that Peterborough would take Darren no later than the third round. One of the kids Darren grew up with and played hockey against was selected as one of the first picks. He looked like a natural to progress to Junior A and the NHL.

We later learned the pressure put on being the first pick is that sometimes you need longer to develop than others. A first pick may have a lot of the basic skills required to play the game but still need the time to develop into a complete hockey player. There is considerable pressure placed on the first pick to be a superstar in his first year of play in Junior A hockey. Some boys take longer to develop both their hockey and life skills. Being away from home and having the adoration of fans is sometimes too much for some of the kids to deal with.

We sat through the first and second round with some anticipation. We knew that Peterborough was planning to take Darren in the third round so we were certain we would be long gone before the end of the

Darren's disappointment over not being picked by Peterborough at the Ontario Hockey League draft was forgotten when he was drafted by the Belleville Bulls.

day. The draft goes until everyone passes on a round, which could be as many as eighteen to twenty rounds.

The third round was announced, and Peterborough had two picks. Peterborough took their turn at the podium. We all tensed up, and then they took someone else. I saw the disappointment on Darren's face. There is not much a parent can do but wait. We knew they had another pick in the third so we felt certain he would go then. They took their next pick, and again, they took someone else. Darren's face told the whole story. We had been led to understand he would be drafted in the third round but there we sat.

However, our disappointment didn't last long. In the next round, the Belleville Bulls picked Darren. This was the beginning of the three years Darren spent in Belleville.

It is funny how you remember things that happen. They leave an impression on you for years to come. The drafts were always a time of excitement and challenge. I have come to the conclusion that there is as much luck involved in the draft as there is skill. I found over the years that the kids who had steady improvement seemed to make it, where as the kids with more natural talent seemed to wash out after a short time.

There is a lot of luck involved in making the NHL. You have to luck into a good Junior team with a good coach who understands what is needed for you to progress as a player. It is difficult to make the transition to a higher level of hockey, and Darren has been fairly good at making the changes required. We knew it would not be easy going to Belleville. They had the biggest ice surface in the Ontario Hockey League. It looked like a frozen Lake Erie. Darren would have to learn to skate better if he was to progress.

Melissa, wearing a Belleville Bulls jersey, and brother Darren.

Belleville

*Darren was
coming into his own
as a player.*

The next three years seemed to fly by. Belleville was a learning experience both for Darren and our family. We began our association with the team at a party that summer. The team owner, Dr. Vaughn, has a large party every July for the entire team from the previous year and invites the draft picks to meet their potential teammates. The prospects of truly making the team are small. Out of the fifteen or sixteen boys drafted five or six will have a real shot at making the team. The rest will be released to play at a lower level. At this age, development is different for all the kids.

The owner of the team was a local doctor who was instrumental in keeping Junior hockey going in the city. It takes a great deal of patience and money to keep a team going. The local fans don't appreciate the effort put forth, but they are quick to complain if a winning team is not produced.

Training Camp
The process for picking the team involves a training camp on the first weekend of September. Darren worked hard that summer to get into shape. He roller-

bladed every day and played all the hockey and base-ball he could. Training camp is not for the weak of mind or heart. We asked a friend of ours what to expect. Darren had talked to another boy who had been to a training camp the year before. We thought we were prepared, but you can never fully understand what goes on until you see it yourself.

The players are divided into three or four teams, and they play against each other. It gives the coaches and scouts a chance to see how the kids do against others of equal size and skill. The older players use it as a test to see if a new player is tough enough. There are usually a lot of fights in training camp because the kids try to show their toughness. The first-round pick is usually signed to play and has a spot in the locker room by the time camp starts. The rest of the kids are trying to get the five or six spots left.

One-third of the team changes every year. The kids are from the ages sixteen to twenty. The chance to play is usually open to the best players, and they move around the league depending on their value. It is unusual for a player to stay with one team for more than one to two years. Most parents have a perception that their little boy will play with one team for three years, then go to a minor team in the American Hockey League, then to the NHL. It rarely happens this way. I know of one parent who demanded a contract with

Darren spent three years on the Junior A Belleville team, five hours from home. Belleville Bulls players (l to r): Greg Dreveny, Brent Gretzky, Craig Fraser, Darren, and Jake Grimes.

a no-trade clause. The coach solves problems like this by not playing the kid. After a while of not dressing or playing, even the parents want him traded. My mother-in-law once told me—be careful for what you ask; it may come true.

I was apprehensive about Darren's ability to make the team. The first choice was Brent Gretzky. He was a smooth player and showed that skill was in the family. The second and third picks also were very good and soon signed. The team was experienced, with three of the players drafted to the NHL Toronto Maple Leafs in the first round the year previous.

We watched as Darren tried to keep up with his skating. He went to a skating instructor the week before camp, hoping to get some help. He was still skating with a wide, choppy stance and no balance at all. If he was hit in the slightest, down he went. He worked hard during the games and didn't back down. Brian Drumm had warned him that the older players would try to intimidate him with threats of a beating if he didn't look out. Scott Thornton was one of the first-round picks of the Toronto Maple Leafs. He and Darren collided a few times in the first scrimmage. I noticed that Darren wouldn't back down from Scott's checks. The last time they collided was in front of the players' bench.

Pretty soon Scott and Darren were in a fight. Junior A allows the players to wear a half face mask, not the full face mask Darren had worn up until then. They exchanged punches and both were connecting, but it was over quickly. The coach liked Darren's scrappiness and signed him to the team. Later some suggested that he made the team because of his ability to fight. Darren will admit that he knew what to do to get on the team, but he also had to learn what to do to stay with the team and play a contributing role.

Billets

Our friend Mike Sadler had warned us the first year would be spent riding the bench and not playing much.

On Canadian Thanksgiving weekend we had a whole group of the family travel to see Darren play in Oshawa. There must have been sixteen of us at the game. Darren didn't get to play and ended up watching the game with us in the stands. There were other times like that, which makes it difficult for a parent. You want to protect your son but you know he has to learn to deal with problems himself if he is to grow as a person.

After signing with the team, Darren needed a place to stay. He was set up with billets who helped him deal with the rigors of playing hockey and being away from home. The billets make sure the players get to their practices and games. Darren was very fortunate to live with many fine families while he played in Belleville.

Not all the kids are as fortunate as Darren was; we have heard many stories about billet problems. I would say that some of the problems are caused by the players themselves and a few times by the billets. Often when these kids move in with a family they have been away from home for a couple of years and have picked up some bad habits.

Adjusting to the First Year

Alcohol is a problem for many of these kids. They are swayed by kids much older, but not always much wiser. Alcohol is part of growing up as a teenager, but the hockey players see it differently than most people. It is given to them wherever they go in town. The sixteen year olds are associating with the twenty year olds so they usually start drinking at an earlier age. I don't think that this exposure is worse than if they were at home, but it does happen and Roberta and I were concerned.

I remember a story about a bar in the Quebec area where the owners had given keys to the players to lock up after they were done drinking. The story is years old and the League has done considerable work to teach the kids how to be responsible adults. In Ontario, the drinking age is nineteen so we came to expect Darren would be tempted by alcohol.

It was in his first year at Belleville that Darren met his future wife. At the time, we felt he had enough to worry about trying to play hockey and go to school without complicating life with a girlfriend. But I will now admit that meeting Cheryl was probably the best thing that could have happened to Darren. Cheryl's family became parents to Darren when we couldn't be there. They added a lot of stability to his life when hockey was so uncertain.

We made a deal with Darren that he would call us after every game if we couldn't make it. Sometimes the call would be at 11:00 PM and sometimes at 4:00 AM. We got used to going back to sleep after the calls, but it was still difficult not being able to attend most of the games. We tried to get to at least every other home game. It was a five-hour drive in good weather with little traffic. We would leave after work on Friday night and drive to Belleville and get in sometime between 10:00 and 11:00. The next day we would go to practice at noon and then to the game that night. After the game we would go out and get pizza with Darren and his friends. The next morning we would drive home.

We made these trips for the better part of three years. When the team got to the end of the regular season, we made the trip every weekend to watch the playoff games. Unfortunately, the first year they did not perform to the expectations of the fans, players, coaches, and management. When the season was done, many of the players left to go home. We felt this was disruptive to school, so we had Darren stay and finish his school year.

Darren had a great setup at school. Peggy Burris was the guidance counselor who was in charge of the hockey players for the Belleville Bulls. The first time I met her I knew she was no nonsense. She looked at Darren and told him to be straight with her and she would help him. If not, he would be in trouble. She was great to deal with. When I became worried about his lack of progress at school, she informed me he was doing everything he could to keep up with being a full-time hockey player and a part-time student. It was

Darren managed to balance being a full-time hockey player and a part-time student, and finished his schooling in Belleville.

because of her that Darren finished his schooling. It took him a year longer than I wanted, but he did it and learned how to manage his time better than before.

Year Two

The next year Darren was much more confident in his ability. He was now an experienced player. Training camp was a time when he got to play the role of the veteran and show the rookies a rough time. He was also coming into his own as a hockey player. The coach of the team changed during the off-season, and Larry Mavity became the coach for Belleville again. Larry was the type of coach Darren could relate to. Again, the luck of being in the right spot at the right time had paid off.

A bonus for Darren was that he was made an assistant captain. He was appreciative of the responsibility as well as the extra time he would get on the ice. It seemed the more he played, the more he molded into a role. Fighting in Junior hockey is a way of weeding out the weak players. I am not talking weak physically, but weak mentally. It doesn't take a strong person to get into a fight, but it does take a strong person to go back out and play after he has been in a fight. Winning a fight is not as important as the idea of "showing up." As the players say, "If you want to watch the game, buy a ticket."

Hockey is a game of intimidation. The real game is played in the minds of the players. I see the mind games that some of the kids play on their opponents, and it is amazing. The thought is not so much what I do, but what you think I will do. In the heat of battle, the mind can play some big games. I was always impressed that Darren learned to finish his check. He always hits the guy with the puck. When a player knows he is going to get hit, he has a tendency to rush his pass or not look where he is passing the puck. If you hit a player every time, he tenses up for the hit. If, every once in a while, you only pretend you are going to hit him, you may have a chance to get the puck.

It takes a tough player to hold the puck just long enough to have someone commit to hitting him before making the pass. I have seen many players who understand the game but are unwilling to make the sacrifice with their body to play it. Most of these people pay to see a National Hockey game now. God-given talent is one thing, but mental toughness is what separates the men from the boys.

Darren's second year, the team was not as good as it had been the year before. They had a tough series in the playoffs and an early end to their season. The end of the regular season is the beginning of the league playoffs. This is an exciting time of the year and our family wanted to be there for as many games as we could. We would travel to the games, usually a five-hour drive, and sometimes we would turn around and drive home after the games.

The end of the hockey season is a time of change for many of the players. They have a farewell party for those who will not be back the following season. A few of the kids stayed in Belleville to complete their year in school but the majority of them moved home to finish school there. Darren stayed in Belleville to complete his school year and played rugby as a way to keep in shape.

His skills had improved a great deal but his skating still needed improvement. The last summer he had gone to a new skating instructor named Laura Stamm. She was able to help him with his skating and the effort showed. We decided he should go back to her again and we hoped he would improve as much as he had before. There is a great deal of work required to change the way a person skates. I think it is better to learn to skate properly at a younger age. We made arrangements for Darren to go back to Laura in Connecticut again during the summer.

A Lesson from the Pros

That summer he worked at a couple of hockey schools and trained for the upcoming year. He also made a trip to California and spent a week with Brent Gretzky at his brother's house. Wayne and a few of the other fellows were getting ready for the Canada Cup games at the time. He came back from the trip and told me he knew he could play pro hockey. The time he spent with these players had convinced him that he could play a pro-style game.

The difference between minor hockey and professional hockey is the speed of the game. The speed difference is not only in skating but the speed required to assess and react to a situation. Darren has told me if you have to think about what to do you are going to

Playing for the Belleville Bulls was a learning experience for Darren.

be on your butt a lot. Skill may play into the equation, but skill without desire and heart will not go very far. Darren was putting a puzzle together with all that he was learning. The knowledge he gained from playing with Wayne Gretzky, Marty McSorley, and others proved to him that he had what it took to play in the NHL.

During this period Darren seemed to be distancing himself from us, but we didn't think this was unusual for he was a teenager. I had hoped we would continue to have a good relationship, but I knew we had to give him some space. Darren always understood he was responsible for his actions, and we couldn't be his watchdog all the time. It was a difficult time for us as a family. He spent little time at home, which I think is normal for most teenagers. And although we didn't always see eye-to-eye, Roberta and I agreed he knew that he would be the person to pay the price for his actions. I remember that I didn't have much guidance growing up and I wanted to help him, but we just didn't communicate well.

The National Hockey League draft that summer was held in Buffalo, and Darren's agent felt he should go to see what to expect. He told Darren that he wouldn't get drafted because he was still considered underage but the experience would do him good. We sat through the first three rounds, and as we had been told, Darren wasn't drafted.

This was the draft in which Eric Lindros was drafted first overall by the Quebec Nordiques and he declined to put the jersey on. Eric had informed the Quebec team that he didn't want them to draft him. By not putting on the sweater, he sent a message that he wouldn't play for them. There were five hundred other kids sitting in the stands with suits on praying for the opportunity that Eric had just passed up. Darren was one of those kids. I know this had an impact on Darren. We left the draft early and were glad we knew what to expect the next year.

The Last Year of Belleville

At the next training camp it became apparent to me that Darren was coming into his own as a player. He was rewarded by being named captain of the team. The disappointing part of the year was the loss of Darren's best friend on the team, Craig Fraser. He was traded to Detroit, which was in our backyard. Craig had become not only Darren's friend but our families had also become close. We found that Craig's parents, Wayne and Faye, were a lot like us. Unfortunately, they lived on the East Coast of Canada, so they couldn't make a lot of the games. But they did make the trip about once a month. That's dedication—to drive sixteen hours to watch a hockey game. When Craig was traded to Detroit, Faye came and spent a few days with us and visited with Craig. We have kept the relationship up to this day and feel lucky to have them as friends.

The year turned into a scoring race for Darren. He was playing with Brent Gretzky, Jake Grimes, and Tony Cimellaro. They were scoring machines. Two years of experience was paying off. That year Darren scored 55 goals and had 72 assists. He was named to the all-star team and traveled to Saskatoon for the all-star game in February. It was there that Darren talked to a couple of agents and informed me he wanted to get a new one. He felt the agent he had was not going to help him get drafted. I had a great relationship with that agent, and do to this day, but unfortunately, he and Darren didn't develop the same type of relationship.

I made a phone call to the agent and told him the bad news. He was a true gentleman and took it well. To this day we recommend him to people. Over the course of the next couple of weeks we talked to three more agents. We listened to what they said and asked ourselves if they were realistic or simply telling us what they thought we wanted to hear.

If an agent comes off as pushy and arrogant, he may have the same problem when dealing with a club. A professional will understand that the player's best interest must be taken into account. Anyone can say no to a deal or yes to a contract. It takes a good agent to understand what is best for his client within the reality of the sport. And Darren chose a good agent.

One of the special treats for Darren and the family that year was a trip to the Memorial Cup held in Seattle in the spring of 1992. Darren was a finalist for Canadian Hockey Player of the Year. Unfortunately he didn't win, but it gave us a chance to visit with him and his grandparents from the West Coast. There were many agents and scouts at the tournament. Many of the players in those games would go on to play in the NHL. But many would not, and it would be the end of their dreams.

It seems that for every boy who gets to have his dream come true there are ten boys who do not get to see their dreams fulfilled. We hoped Darren would get his chance. There was a dinner for the players and the guests. Darren and the other two boys nominated were introduced. The boy from the Quebec League, Charles Poulin, was the winner. The other boy was from the Western League, and his name was Cory Hirsch. It was an honor for Darren to be nominated, and as the representative of the Ontario Hockey League, he was their Player of the Year.

Preparing for the Draft

Darren had done everything he could to make a name for himself in the Ontario Hockey League. It was now time for the agent to do what he could to make Darren more attractive. The draft that year was in Montreal, and the whole family was excited about the prospect of Darren getting drafted. We also knew there were three teams who were interested and had set up interviews.

As he had for the past two years, Darren went to a skating school in Darien, Connecticut. The school was instructed by Laura Stamm. Laura stood only 4' 11" but she knew her skating. Within five minutes of arriving, she had Darren working on a different stride. She just told him he had to continue to practice and he would get better. The mechanics of skating are fairly straightforward, but it is a difficult task to make all the components come together and still try to move a puck around or avoid a check. You have to continually work on your skating and practice your drills as if you are under game conditions.

The draft in Montreal was the week after the power skating so Darren and I drove to Connecticut for the school with intention of driving on to Montreal for the draft. We knew of three teams interested in Darren and had expected him to be taken in the third or lower round.

A twenty year old is drafted later because the under-age eighteen and nineteen year olds have to go in the first three rounds. The year previous Darren would

Instructor Laura Stamm helped Darren improve his skating.

have been considered an underage player for the NHL draft and only eligible for the first three rounds. With him now being twenty, he was eligible for all rounds but history had shown us that the younger players were taken first.

The drive to Connecticut was full of excitement. We were excited about the draft and thought about the twenty-six teams Darren could end up on. Would he go to a team that would give him a chance to learn how to play a pro game? Or would he get stuck in an organization that didn't care about the player? I know it seems strange to think that teams don't care about the players, but look at the track record of some of the high draft picks. They are brought on too quickly and then they lose their confidence. I have listened to many stories of players who have been drafted high and never made it to the NHL. I have also heard of players who were never drafted and made the transition through plain hard work. I think it is a blessing not to be the first draft pick. There are no preconceived ideas about making an immediate impact. If a player is drafted late, he is marked as being a low draft pick and possibly not very good.

Once we got to Connecticut Roberta called. She said word had reached her that the Detroit Red Wings were sending a scout to look at Darren skate at the skating school. This was the first indication we had that they were interested in Darren. Mike Adessa was from the Boston area. He drove down to see Darren and me in Connecticut. Mike introduced himself and then excused himself to watch in silence as Darren was put through a one-hour skate. After the drill was done, Mike asked if he could take us out for lunch. Darren quickly showered and off we went.

There was a little fast-food restaurant down the road that Darren and I had become accustomed to eating in. The three of us sat there for the next two hours and talked. Mike wanted to know about our family, who we were and what we thought would happen in the draft. He also asked about the other teams Darren had talked to. I was straight with him and told him about all the conversations we had had over the past two months. Both Darren and I liked Mike, he had a way of making you feel at ease. He also was very direct.

Mike asked Darren if he had the desire to play in the National Hockey League. He didn't have to ask twice. Darren responded that he would do whatever he could to play. Mike informed us the word among the other scouts was Darren's skating was not up to par for the NHL. Fortunately Mike felt that Darren had enough ability and desire to overcome his skating shortfall.

The Draft

Darren assured me
he had the desire
to play in the NHL—
he would do anything
they asked of him
to make the team.

After Darren and I had our lunch with Mike, we left for Montreal. Mike told us to enjoy the moment and not worry because things would work out. The drive gave me a chance to talk to Darren about the conversation that Mike and I had regarding Darren's desire. Darren assured me he had the desire to play in the NHL as it had been his dream from the time he was five. He would do anything they asked of him to make the team.

The trip took about six hours so we got into Montreal late at night. Melissa and Roberta had arrived earlier on the train. More of the family would arrive the day before the draft. I think there were about twenty-five people from home plus Cheryl and her parents. The Belleville team had good representation because they had three or four players who were going to get drafted. The next three days were a series of meetings. The teams would interview players to get a feel for the kids before drafting them.

The Interview Process

There is a lot of luck involved in sports, both good and bad. We would go from hotel to hotel and wait for

Darren to be interviewed. Sitting in the lobbies of these hotels was very interesting. I guess it is safe to say that the managers, scouts, and team executives of some of the teams are not nice people. Some talk about people in the open regardless of who is in the area. They have few people skills and are in a constant battle to maintain whatever power they hold. I always wondered what some of them saw in certain players, and I was surprised to find out many have very little knowledge about the player and his game. The person making the decision to draft a boy may have only met him for five minutes or not at all. Some teams won't interview a player if they want to throw other teams off about their interest.

Darren's agents had arranged for us to meet with three teams and then meet with them. We felt the team with the most interest was Toronto and thought they would take Darren as early as the third round. Darren was rated in the top seventy-five players, and we were confident he would get drafted high enough for a team to have an interest in trying to develop him. We knew the next year would be a change for the family. The drives to Belleville were over, and the anticipation of where Darren would play next was already on our minds.

The night before the draft, Darren's agents had a party for the draft picks, and many NHL past and present stars showed up. We walked around in awe of the people in attendance. The evening was full of excitement for both the players and the teams. I am always amazed at the talk among the team representatives. I saw two fellows have a heated debate about a player within earshot of the player and his family. They didn't recognize the player, and they didn't care who heard their stories. The poor kid just stood there and kept his mouth shut. These two guys didn't have enough class to stop even when they were told the young man could hear them.

The Day Begins

I had a meeting with one of Darren's agents later that night. He told me the interest in Darren was good, and he felt he could go as high as the third round. The next morning we were all up and dressed before 8:00 AM. Darren dressed in a suit. Most of us were too nervous to eat breakfast. Off we went to the Montreal Forum. There is a buzz around a draft that is very hard to explain. Many of the kids there have a great deal of nervous energy. This is a moment in a young man's life where he will be placed on the auction block for all to see. A lot of parents were going around with a "my son is better than your son" attitude. The agents were trying to tie up loose ends and still sign players to representation contracts. Some of the seedier agents were trying to get players to switch agents. Many of the players were from Europe, and this was their first exposure to the draft and pro hockey.

The draft is exciting. Many of the teams do a lot of trading to change their position in the draft. It is believed that a good draft can set up a team for years to come. It can also do the opposite if a player, or players, don't work out. The teams usually have a book of the players and the possible spot in the draft they should go. They also have in-depth charts of their own needs and requirements. Sometimes the coaches have input into what type of player the team should be looking for. Many times the person making the final decision has little knowledge about the prospects and will select the highest not-yet-drafted player. I am sure the teams could save a lot of money if they would just put a bunch of names in a hat and draw them out.

Scouts

I know many of the teams want you to think they have done a lot of work, and most of them do. Scouting in hockey is a network of old boys, some of whom are very good at their jobs. However, there are a few who don't act very professional in regard to their evaluation of players. Over the years, I have overheard conversations where a scout will simply take the word of someone else about a player and his abilities. Others will compare notes about a player's potential and then tell a different scout what they were just told.

As Roberta says, "It takes a couple of bad apples to spoil the barrel." But I don't want to paint all scouts with the same brush. I would be remiss if I left you with the impression that all scouts are bad. In fact, the majority of pro scouts work very hard. They sometimes see a game a night in cities hundreds of miles apart. They are on the road constantly, which is not conducive to a family life. Most of the scouts have played the game and understand it takes more than skill to play in the NHL. I noticed that if a scout was a mediocre player, he seemed to have a better eye for talent. I guess it is all that time on the bench.

I should also mention that some of the best scouts never played in the NHL, and some don't even play hockey. They have become students of the game and, best of all, good judges of character. It takes talent to get you to the NHL, but it will take character to keep you there. There are hundreds of kids playing in the minors who, with the right breaks, will play in the NHL. It is like the housing market: "location, location, location." If you don't end up with a team, coach, general manager, or fellow players who fit the type of player you are, it is difficult to overcome the adversity. Our test was to come.

"With Their Second Pick, the Detroit Red Wings Select . . ."

The first round took forever. Every team can take up to fifteen minutes between picks. I was amazed when the second and third picks had to have a discussion about who to take. If you haven't worked through the possible combinations for the first two or three, how will you decide later? Some teams have a point system, and some draft according to the stars (that's how it seems anyway). We sat through the first round with few surprises. Because we were not expecting Darren to be picked until the third or later rounds, there was little pressure on us. Some of the kids who had been highly rated had slipped, and the Europeans had come in earlier than expected.

When the Maple Leafs landed two picks in the first round we felt there was an outside chance that Darren would end up as one of those picks. But that didn't happen. Detroit had their second pick in the draft in the second round. Their first pick was Curtis Bowen of the Ottawa 67's. He was a big center who was a year younger than Darren. With their second pick, Detroit announced they would select the right wing from the Belleville Bulls, Darren McCarty. We were ecstatic and jumped up out of our seats with joy. Our hearts stopped while Darren walked, or should I say ran, to the Red Wings' table and put on the shirt with the famous winged wheel. We watched with pride as he shook hands with everyone at the Detroit table and then motioned us down to be with him.

We were introduced to all the scouts and the management of the team. Then the family, with Darren wearing his new team's jersey, was taken for pictures. We will always cherish that picture and the treatment we received that day. We were soon joined by the rest of our family and friends, including Cheryl and her family. We decided to have a party. Back to the hotel we went to ask if they had a room we could use. By now it was mid-afternoon, and the draft was still going strong.

The Celebration

The hotel decided the best place for us was a banquet room that was not being used. The champagne flowed and toasts were said by all. I watched as the family enjoyed the moment. We also were aware that some of Darren's teammates were not yet picked. We hoped they would be drafted so we could all have a party together.

Two of Darren's teammates, Brent Gretzky and Jake Grimes, were also drafted. Brent went to Tampa Bay and Jake went to Ottawa. We were pleased that they could join in the celebration along with their friends and family. The celebration was made extra special

Belleville's team owner, Dr. Robert Vaughn, and Belleville coach, Larry Mavity, were on hand to celebrate with Darren when he was drafted by the Red Wings in 1992.

when the coach of Belleville, Larry Mavity, and the Belleville team owner, Dr. Vaughn, joined in. I would say there were about fifty to sixty of us in this room. The festivity of the evening was just beginning. Everyone had a little too much to drink and some were calling it an early evening. About eight of us decided we would continue at a bar. We sat around and relished the events of the day. The bars closed at 2:00 AM in Montreal and we knew we had a long drive ahead of us the next morning. It was a cool summer night as we prepared to walk the streets of Montreal back to our hotel for a couple of hours of sleep.

As we were about to leave the bar, Darren went up to a member of the management team from St. Louis and introduced himself as Darren McCarty, a Detroit Red Wing. We knew the journey was just starting. I know the family wished him well, but we felt the NHL was still some time away. It was our hope that the Red Wings would sign him to a contract and allow him a couple of years to develop in the minors. The summer went pretty quickly, because training camp was only two and a half months away. Darren worked hard to get into shape. He played hockey in Sarnia on Sunday evenings against some of the pros who had started a summer league to keep in shape.

We were still pinching ourselves the next morning when we left for our twelve-hour drive home. Of all the teams in the league, Darren was drafted by the team closest to our home. We knew the challenge of making the next jump to the NHL was still to come, but we now believed that Darren had a chance to make it. Some slept on the way home, but most of us talked about the draft and the coming season, and what it would bring. We started to look at Detroit's lineup to see where Darren would fit in. If you look at the team they had, it would appear there was no room. But changes happen quickly in the NHL, and the makeup of a team can be changed almost immediately.

The next year would prove to be difficult for everyone in the family. Darren would be tested as a player, and his family values would be tested. Darren's grandfather, Bob, found out he had cancer. Darren was very close to his grandfather and they shared a special bond. We were concerned about Bob, and Darren had his hands full trying to play in the American Hockey League.

The American Hockey League

*It is difficult for a family
to lose contact with a son or daughter
when they go away.
You have to trust your children
to allow them the opportunity
to learn as you have learned.*

The American Hockey League was made up of the minor league teams for the National Hockey League. The Detroit Red Wings have a minor team in Glens Falls, New York. The Adirondack Red Wings played on the East Coast of the United States and in Canada, with the closest game to us in Hamilton, Ontario. We knew Darren would be going there after training camp. He would get a couple of exhibition games in and then make the trip to Glens Falls.

Contract Negotiations

We still had not reached an agreement with the Red Wings about a contract for Darren. Contracts are like chess games. Each party plays their moves very deliberately waiting for the other to blink. Darren went to training camp with no contract and took out an insurance policy should he get hurt. Darren's agent explained this was normal and told him not to worry. He didn't have to be under contract unless they decided to keep him. The team doesn't have to sign him, but they take the chance he might go to another team without compensation the next year.

The training camp was being held in Flint, Michigan, at a facility that houses two arenas. The people of Flint were avid hockey fans, and a chance to see their Red Wing team brought them out in masses. The players are divided into three teams with a game played between two of them each day while the other team is practicing and doing drills. Training camp is not for the faint of heart. Darren was in a couple of fights the first day. Everyone is out to prove they belong. The veterans have to show the rookies that the team is going to be hard to make. Most teams try to have a mix of veteran players with some new ones thrown in. It takes a while to develop, and the Red Wings were a good team with many great players when Darren arrived.

The team was full of good returning players, and Darren tried as best he could to make a good impression. Traditionally, the Toronto rookies play a game against the Red Wing rookies. This game was in Brantford, and we made the trip to see the game. As usual, the game was a series of fights mixed with some scrambled hockey. After the game a good portion of both teams went to the minors. Darren would get to play an exhibition game against the Montreal team. He played well and even got to start the game. It was a show of class to let the rookie start. After the game he was informed he would be sent to Glens

Falls for the balance of the year. He was told to work hard and that he would be called up if there were any injuries.

Darren still did not have a contract with the Red Wings. His agent informed us the team was not willing to spend the money so it appeared Darren would be playing for another team for that year. There were a couple of teams in the International League he could play for and get paid a good salary. He would then go back in the draft if he and Detroit could not reach an agreement. The last Friday in September we left Leamington to drive to Glens Falls with the hope of seeing Darren play. If he did not sign with the team, his agent had given us instructions to bring him back home. We knew the team was playing out of town and the bus was leaving at 3:00 PM for the game. Darren was on the bus saying goodbye to the team when he was notified that the Red Wings had called and agreed to the contract. We received word from Darren's agent just as we were getting ready to cross the bridge at Fort Erie. It was still a six-hour drive from there to Glens Falls.

Letting Go

The people of Glens Falls are definitely lucky. Upstate New York is picturesque and has golf, skiing, hiking, and many little shops for browsing. We fell in love with the area and made plans to make the trip once a month. Fortunately the team played on Saturday night so we got a chance to see games when we were there. We also made trips to Hamilton, Ontario; Rochester, New York; New Haven, Connecticut; and Hershey, Pennsylvania. My brother was living in New Jersey so he got to see Darren play in Hershey, Baltimore, and New Haven. It was good the family could see him play.

It is difficult for a family to lose contact with a son or daughter when they go away. We had the experience of Darren moving away from home to play hockey at the age of sixteen but the move to Glens Falls was traumatic. The five-hour drives to Belleville were replaced with ten-hour drives. We worried about Darren as he would be living with others his own age without the benefit of a billet.

You have to trust your children to allow them the opportunity to learn as you have learned. We didn't have the benefit of having our parents around to always guide us. I know we also didn't have the type of lifestyle which hockey players have or the disposable income to spend. This is a time to trust the values you have instilled in them. I wouldn't say it is easy and I will say we did worry that he would get sidetracked but Darren was very aware that he would be the person who would pay the price if there were problems.

A Family Reunion

Darren's grandfather was not doing well. He had not had a chance to see Darren play in the American Hockey League. We decided to try a trip to Glens Falls by plane with Grandpa and Grandma, Roberta, Melissa, and me. We went to the airport and were informed our flight to Albany had been cancelled. My wife was a travel agent, and we knew Darren's grandfather would back out if we had to wait in the airport for another flight. My wife explained our plight to a person from the airline. She got us on a flight to Syracuse, New York, which still meant a drive of three hours, but it got us to our destination. We got in about two in the morning, and there was Darren at the hotel waiting for us. His grandfather was grateful to see him. Unfortunately, Bob had left medical supplies he needed on the plane we were supposed to fly on. I left at 7:00 am for the airport in Albany to retrieve the luggage. Everyone was happy to see me, and it taught me to never fly with anything I was not prepared to lose.

The weekend went well and was uneventful from that point on. We felt fortunate that Bob was able to make the trip. This would be the only time he would get to see Darren play in the American Hockey League. The cancer was consuming Bob and he never did see Darren play in the NHL. The season was over and Darren came home for a while. It became apparent that Bob was failing. My wife spent as much time with her father as possible. I was not as aware of the seriousness of Bob's illness. I now appreciate what a courageous person he was.

Unfortunately, Bob lost his battle with cancer in July of 1993. I am glad I was able to be with him and the family in his final moments. In retrospect, I learned a great deal from Bob. He taught me that death with dignity can be achieved if you work at it. He never felt sorry for himself nor did he blame anyone for his plight. His approach would be a great example for me later. Darren gave his grandfather a puck to go to the grave with. This was his first goal as a professional hockey player. I am sure that Darren would have been proud to have his grandfather see him play in the NHL, but it didn't happen. We do know that Bob looks out for Darren, and we are assured they communicate.

The National Hockey League

We had come to understand
over the past year that hockey
for a professional hockey player
is not a labor of work,
but a labor of love.

The next year the Red Wings made a few roster changes so the chance of Darren making the team improved. Training camp was held in Detroit, and we fully expected Darren to play in a couple of exhibition games then be sent back to Glens Falls. It seemed like the trigger would fall many times. He stuck through the training camp and the exhibition season with the team. He was told if he kept up the hard work, he had a remote chance of making the team. Playing with the Detroit Red Wings was a great thrill. We watched in awe as our son skated around with people like Steve Yzerman, Paul Coffey, and Bob Probert. Darren had to take the approach of doing what he had to do to make the team. Fighting was what he felt would get him noticed and hopefully secure a spot on the roster.

His reputation soon grew as a player who would look out for the other members on his team. You realize as a parent when your son gets in a fight that he may get hurt. It does take a while to become accustomed to the fisticuffs and even when you see it happen your heart does a skip.

There is an electricity in the stands when two play-ers square off. We feel it is better to drop the gloves and fight it out rather than see a player use a stick like a weapon. I will say the first time Darren fought Marty McSorley we were worried. The years in the OHL and the year in the American Hockey League had tempered us but this was a true seasoned veteran and Darren was just a rookie. He held his own with Marty, and we felt from then on that Darren could take care of himself.

Year One, 1993-94

In mid-October the team informed Darren that he could find a place to live in Detroit and that he was to stay with the Red Wings rather than be sent back to Adirondack. This meant he could settle down, and he and Cheryl planned a wedding in the spring. There was a time during the All-Star break when he had a weekend free so a wedding was planned. We were thrilled as Cheryl was a great addition to the family. She was part of the family since Darren had played in Belleville his first year. She had been a great support for him over the last four years and her parents, Lynn and Norm Richards, had also become good friends.

The wedding was set to be held in Belleville, Ontario, in the United Church. It was good to see all the people who had helped Darren get to this point in his career. Craig Fraser was Darren's best man and flew in from Nova Scotia for the wedding. Hockey makes it difficult to keep up with your friends other than by phone calls and the hope of playing in a city close enough to have them visit.

I can understand how people that play hockey together develop lifelong friendships. You eat, sleep, travel, and live with twenty-five others for nine months of the year. You develop a close association with your teammates.

The season was a great learning experience for Darren as he was learning the pressures and the requirements to play professional hockey. You have to be willing to pay the price to stay, with your body by checking people or dropping to block a shot, and by biding your time for a chance to play. Mentally, you have to always be in the game even if you only get a few shifts. The hardest part of the game is in your head. You must decide if this is truly what you want and prepare to pay the price to stay no matter what you have to do.

Fighting may have got Darren on the team but he had to develop his other skills if he was to stay. He would stay after practice for an hour to work on his skating and stick-handling. As the season progressed he was improving and getting more playing time.

The season turned out to be a disappointment for the team. They were eliminated by the San Jose Sharks in the first round of the playoffs. I never realized the amount of people involved in running a team. It was sad seeing the disappointment on the faces of all the personnel in the arena after that last game. The players were very competitive and took the loss hard. This loss was used as a fire to motivate them for the next year. Darren finished the season with 67 games played, 9 goals, 17 assists, and 181 minutes in penalties. He felt he was on his way to securing a spot on one of the original six teams in the NHL.

After the season was over Darren got invited to Sweden to practice for two weeks with the Swedish Hockey Association players. He felt the early practice before camp would give him an edge on the players for the upcoming camp in the fall. He spent two weeks in August doing hard workouts with the Swedish players. They combine rigid dry land training with on-ice drills.

Darren worked hard to make this training pay off for himself. He was proving he was willing to pay the price to play in the NHL.

Year Two, 1994-95

Darren's second year was shortened because of the lockout or strike. It all depends on which side of the fence you were sitting on as to what you called it. All we knew was Darren and the rest of his team were not playing hockey. They tried to practice as best they could without making it too formal.

118

Melissa and Roberta show off an octopus thrown onto the ice during the 1994 playoffs.

It was difficult for the players as they had been conditioned for almost twenty years to play hockey in the fall, winter, and spring. I know as a parent we had become accustomed to hearing the sound of skates cutting through the ice during these seasons. It had become a fall tradition to attend training camp and see who the new players would be for the team.

Fortunately, Darren was occupied with his love of golf but once the winter arrived that had to be put on hold. We had come to understand over the past year that hockey for a professional hockey player is not a labor of work, but a labor of love. I think most of them would play for nothing, but as long as players are getting paid they should get as much as they can during their career. I was once told the average career of a NHL player is five years. The players who play only one season or part of a season are balanced by the players who have a ten-year career.

The players were out of their natural rhythm for the season and it showed. There were some benefit games but the longer the season was delayed the worse it looked for the league starting up. We were worried as both parents and fans that the season would be missed with the labor dispute and that a missed season would be one year shorter for Darren's career and his fellow players.

Fortunately the season began in the late winter and the players were ready to get going as soon as the ink was dry on the new contract.

With it being a short season each game held importance. A loss meant much more in the shortened season than it had during a regular 82-game schedule. I remembered the disappointing end of the year last year and the impact on the Red Wing franchise. It was sad to think of the people in the arena who had not worked over the labor dispute. The season finally started on January 20th.

The life of a professional athlete is not all the glamour that it appears to be. Most people think the players play a few games a week and have the occasional practice. There is practice every day with a game day skate thrown in. There are many games on the road with extended trips. I have explained to people that the life of a professional hockey player is difficult because you know the day to start work is in the fall but the last day of work is the day you are eliminated from the playoffs. In between you have to work seven days a week. Once most people hear this I think it takes the shine off being a professional hockey player.

The season ended with the Red Wings beating the San Jose Sharks in the first round. In the second round they defeated the Dallas Stars to go on to play the Chicago Blackhawks for the Western Conference

Finals. Once they defeated Chicago the Red Wings played the New Jersey Devils for the Stanley Cup.

There was a great deal of anticipation for the team to do well against New Jersey but it was not to happen.

The first two games were played in Detroit with New Jersey winning both the games. New Jersey played a very defensive game with puck control, which seemed to stymie the Red Wings. After two games the series went to New Jersey. The team had been very confident and felt they could win both games there to bring the series back to Detroit. Unfortunately it didn't turn out that way and New Jersey went on to win both games and the Stanley Cup. I remember the players were very upset about losing. In years to come the loss may have been what helped them learn how to win. You have to learn to win as well as learn to accept defeat. You can't let the highs of a victory or the lows of a loss overshadow the job at hand. You must maintain a professional attitude in all games regardless of what has happened in the last game.

Darren ended the year with 5 goals, 8 assists, and 88 penalty minutes in a shortened season. The team had played well but the goal of a Stanley Cup had eluded them again.

A Turn for the Worst

That summer, Roberta and I were in Toronto for a meeting. During the meeting, I felt a sharp pain in my

Teammates Kris Draper and Chris Osgood with Darren at the 1995 playoffs.

Darren on the bench.

chest. Fearing a problem, I drove home and went to the hospital. Now, that drive is three hours so I didn't tell my wife until we were going past our house on the way to the hospital. She still reminds me what a stubborn person I am. I guess Darren inherited some of my traits. The hospital thought it was a heart attack so they kept me in overnight. The local doctor told me there was nothing wrong with my heart, but there was something wrong with my blood.

I was scheduled to see a hematologist a few weeks later. I wasn't worried because they didn't seem to be concerned. I was to learn more over the next few months. I had a bone marrow sample taken, and it proved to be negative. The doctor informed me I had a disease called monoclonal gamopathy of undetermined significance. It was, in itself, a mouthful to say. A good friend of mine who is a doctor sat down with me and explained what the disease was. He informed me that it was a good thing that the test was negative. It wasn't good that I had an output of protein in my urine. This disease would eventually turn into a disease called multiple myeloma. I had cancer. I read everything I could about the disease, and the prognosis was not good.

The average age of discovery of the disease is sixty-five and the average life expectancy after discovery is twenty-four months. I was forty-six and devastated. All

I could think of was the terrible death of my father-in-law, Bob. Cancer was a death sentence, and I was walking to the gallows. I had to see another doctor, and I had a kidney biopsy done. This was positive for a disease called amyloidosis. Again, this disease is rare and there is no cure. At least I had been tested and my bone marrow was negative.

I went through a period of three months where I would go to my office and go through the motions. I had no interest in work, and I would go home and go back to bed some days. The thoughts that ran through my head were destructive. My wife and family life were suffering. I felt sorry for myself. My concern was that I had a daughter and son who I would not get to see continue to grow up. I was concerned about how Roberta would manage without me. I wasn't being very strong.

During the first week of December my wife and I were on a trip to Arizona and had the chance to sit and talk. The fear I was experiencing was the fear of the unknown. I was afraid of things I had no control over. She told me that whatever the outcome, she would be with me. Over the past couple of years this conversation has given me great comfort. I understand how people can feel about having cancer and I know the outcome may not be good, but I do feel that my wife will support me no matter what happens. It was more difficult talking to our children about my disease.

I wanted to share with them what I was going through but also wanted to protect them from my problems.

More Tests

I was scheduled for another bone marrow biopsy in January. This time it came back positive for the cancer cells. I was certainly not happy about this, but I felt confident that I would handle it better than I had been. My friend Dr. Murray O'Neil was again a great deal of help to me. He called the last doctor I had worked with and asked him what he was going to do to help me. Murray asked him what he would do if it were a member of his family who was sick. The doctor explained that he would find the best medical advice possible and get them there. Murray, being the old-time country doctor he is, used this and asked the doctor if his patients should not be treated the same as family. The doctor agreed. Now we had to find a specialist in amyloidosis. It took about a month to find a specialist, who was in Boston. I received an appointment for the first of April.

The local cancer clinic started me on chemotherapy, which consisted of pills for four days then steroids for four days. The steroids were killers. I would bloat up like a balloon, and I couldn't sleep at night. I had gone through two courses of the chemotherapy by the time I was scheduled to go to Boston. I contacted the

Ontario Medical Insurance group to find out if they would pay for the trip to Boston, since there are no specialists in Canada. There are good and bad things about socialized medicine. I was told to send in an application, which would take three to six months to process. If I was in danger of dying, I could go at my own expense and then apply to see if it would be covered. This is the approach I used. It cost us over $8,000, and I did, after a year, get back eighty percent of my expenses.

The clinic in Boston reviewed the findings from Windsor and did their own testing. After three days of testing they decided I didn't have amyloidosis but said I should get back home as soon as possible. My blood counts were so low it was dangerous for me to travel. I should have known there was a problem. I was so tired all the time, and I could barely walk without being out of breath. The clinic suggested I go through something called a stem cell transplant. They also said the best place to get one in Canada was at the University of Toronto Hospital.

The thought of undergoing a transplant was pretty scary. I went over to Detroit and had lunch with Darren one day after practice. We had not told him the full extent of what was going on, and I felt this was something that we had to do. I laid out to him what the doctors had said. We talked about what would happen if

I became too ill or died. He told me not to worry, but I still worried.

Tough Choices

Multiple myeloma is a disease of the blood and the bone. Once it is going strong, it is difficult to slow it down and stop it. Most cancer centers were looking at stem cell transplants as a method of treatment. The transplant would not put the cancer into a complete remission, but it could slow the disease down. The idea is to treat the disease as aggressively as possible while a person's health is reasonable. A donor transplant was ruled out for several reasons. A match would have to be found, and there are many more rejections than matches. The mortality rate with allogenic, or donor, transplants is in the thirty percent range. The mortality of the stem cell, or autologous, transplants, which use your own cells instead of a donor's, is in the five percent or lower range. I decided to go for this method. I was concerned about my brother or sister living with the idea that their bone marrow had failed in me. They were tested, but I had already made my mind up before it came back that neither one of them was a match.

Many things go through your mind when you are sick. Sometimes the disease is not as bad as the treatment. This is the case for multiple myeloma. My chemotherapy changed to a type where I had to go into the hospital. I had a tube placed into my chest, which would feed the chemicals directly into a main blood supply. If they tried to put it into a vein through a normal IV, the veins would plug up. The treatment would last four days and I would need three treatments before they would see if I was able to have the transplant. The idea is to get the cancer counts down as low as possible to allow the transplant to work. Chemotherapy is like killing an ant with an atom bomb. It kills off everything. I was not worried about losing my hair, but I was unprepared for the mood swings the high doses of steroids caused. When I was in treatment, I would stay in the hospital, and I could get around with the IV pole tagging along. There was a nice area during the day where I could take a book and read or take my computer and work. I tried to maintain my work, but I soon found it to be too difficult.

I would go from sleeping all the time to staying awake for three or four days, depending on where I was in the cycle of treatment. My weight increased, and I had a red puffy look to my already short-for-my-weight frame. I was now over 240 pounds on a 5' 7" frame. I was constantly out of breath and not the easiest person to be around. My wife decided to take some time off from her job as manager of a travel agency. This was great because she was able to spend time with me each day when I was in the hospital and was able to go with me to my doctor appointments. It was amazing that we would sit in a meeting with a doctor and each hear something completely different. We started to take notes and compiled a book to keep the notes in. This book proved to be very valuable.

The hospital for the transplant was in Toronto, which meant we would have to travel 250 miles for each visit to the doctor. On my first trip to Toronto I met my new doctor. Keith Stewart is a great guy who has the compassion of a saint. To me, he was a lifesaver. We discussed the options I had, and I gave him the "what would you do if this was you" speech. Usually when you ask a doctor this, he or she gives you a song and dance about how the decision is up to you and how he or she shouldn't put forth personal ideas. Keith told me exactly what he would do if it were him. He told me to go home and review my options since I still had two more treatments to go through before he could tell if I was going to be able to have the transplant.

When I had been in Boston, they were doing transplants for the treatment of amyloidosis. They used the stem cell transplant, or rescue, and added the use of a machine called a cell separator to clean up the cell from the diseased cells. The technology was in its infancy, but a company in the States was doing a study which I could participate in if I wanted. The idea of cleaning my own blood and putting it back into my body appealed to both Roberta and me. Unfortunately, with a study there are guidelines that must be followed. Fifty percent of the people get the machine, and the others don't. They wait and watch the patients over a five-year period and then recommend whether the procedure or medicine is an improvement. I have nothing against clinical trials and I know they are important, but we felt I should get the use of the machine if possible. It would not be covered under the current medical system we had in Canada so we agreed to pay for the use of the machine.

The study would also use only chemotherapy and no full-body radiation. When I talked to Keith, he recommended the radiation but couldn't give me an opinion about the stem cell separator. I was concerned that I would not get the machine, and by the time I found out it was beneficial, I would be too sick to go through another transplant. The machine use would cost us $12,000, but we both felt the gamble was worth it.

Year Three, 1995-96

Darren went to Europe again in the summer to work on his skating and conditioning. It had become evident the extra work had paid off in the last year so it was anticipated the next season would be a breakout year for Darren and the team. They had built a good framework the past season and the disappointment of the loss to New Jersey seemed to make them hungrier this year.

This was the year the Russian Five were put together. It seemed they were magicians with the puck and could play at will with their opponents. I watched in amazement as they would work the opposition into a hypnotic trance. The Russian Five would do passing plays that were similar to the Harlem Globetrotters. The puck appeared as if on a string with the Russians controlling the cord.

The team was winning almost every game they played in. They were on a record streak to win more games than any team had in the NHL. The season couldn't move quickly enough for the fans. They felt this team was the team to bring the Stanley Cup to Detroit and stop a streak of bad luck. It was great for the team players but it was extra special for the Illitch family. They had purchased the team when any win was cause for celebration and worked their magic in getting the players and coaching staff to the point where they would win on a consistent basis.

The end of the year brought the team to a total of 62 wins. As fans, we felt assured of them winning the Stanley Cup. I was always told there are two seasons to a hockey schedule—the regular season and then the playoffs. We have learned that the playoffs are different from the rest of the year. The intensity is greater and the outcome of every game is important.

The 62-game win was a record which would be hard to match in the modern NHL.

The playoffs started with a hard-fought series against the Winnipeg Jets. The Jets were already making a move to Phoenix so they played extra hard for the local Winnipeg fans. The games were tough but the Red Wings won round one and moved on to play the St. Louis Blues. The games were very exciting due to the Blues' addition of Wayne Gretzky as an end of the year pickup. The most exciting game was a double overtime with Steve Yzerman scoring the winning goal.

The next opponent was the Colorado Avalanche. This series was very difficult and the Red Wings seemed to falter. The effort that had won them a record amount of games that year didn't seem to work in this playoff series. There seemed to be a lapse of skill right when winning meant everything. Colorado had the Red Wings' number and won the series to eliminate the team again. We had been close but not close enough. The fans seemed to think the team was jinxed and wanted a winner. There was talk of wholesale changes but the owners and the coaching staff didn't make any major changes.

Darren finished the year with 15 goals, 14 assists, and 158 minutes in penalties.

Defeated again: the Red Wings faced off against the Colorado Avalanche in the 1996 playoffs.

A New McCarty

Cheryl and Darren were expecting their first child. With the team in the playoffs, it would have been difficult for Cheryl to have the baby when Darren could be there. They decided to induce the baby's birth for a time between games.

I was going through my last chemotherapy treatment and then had to go to Toronto for an evaluation. Since we were expecting to be away for up to three months, we awaited the arrival of our new grandchild with great anticipation. After one of the playoff games against Colorado, Cheryl and Darren went to the hospital and Cheryl was induced.

Griffin James Robert McCarty was born into the world on May 20, 1996. We went to the hospital that afternoon to see him and I was amazed at how little he was. I was never good with kids, but I was beaming with pride as I watched Darren hold his son.

Mac

During my next visit to the hospital for chemotherapy, I dislodged the tube in my chest. The doctors X-rayed the tube to see if it had come out of the blood supply. They noticed a spot on the end of the tube, which was a growth. The tube would have to come out. A doctor came in my room and removed the tube. They just removed the stitches, which held it in place, and gave

Darren became a father in 1996, when his son, Griffin, was born.

it a pull. My wife picked me up on Saturday morning, and I told her I wanted to go see Darren and Cheryl, but more than that my new grandson. We also took my new best friend, Mac.

When I was first diagnosed, my office staff decided I needed a companion. They talked my wife into letting me get a dog. They even gave me the money to buy him. Darren had a golden retriever named Jake. I spent time with him and thought he was great. My wife was reluctant about us having a dog but agreed it would keep me company when I was home, which was more than ever. I had gone from working all day to being home all day. We got our golden retriever the week before Christmas, and he became part of the family. The day I was to leave the hospital was in May, and Mac was almost six months old. He was thin and still had that puppy odor. Having been in the hospital for the past week, I missed him a great deal.

We went over and spent the afternoon with Darren, Cheryl, and Griffin. Jake and Mac played in the yard. Things were going pretty well. I was tired so we didn't stay too long. Once we got home all I wanted to do was sleep.

A Late Night Scare

I went to bed about 10:00. At about 2:00 AM I woke up sweating. I took off my pajamas and tried to go back to sleep. The next thing I remember was trying to get out of bed to go to the bathroom. I fell and got up to get to the bathroom. Once I got to the bathroom I fell again. I was burning up and drifted in and out of consciousness. My wife heard the commotion and came to find me passed out on the floor.

She called for an ambulance and sat with me until they arrived. Once they arrived, they got me on a stretcher and took me to the local hospital. During the trip to the local hospital, the attendant, who I knew, was talking to me to try to keep me awake. I remember passing a building and thinking "what an interesting view." When they got me to the hospital in Leamington, I had a blood pressure of 60/40 with an 104-degrees Fahrenheit temperature. I was going into shock. I remember lying on a table in an emergency room with people running in and out, sticking IV lines in me and talking to me. Fortunately, my wife had taken the book I kept all my notes in, and she gave it to the ER doctor.

The ER doctor called the cancer clinic and told the attending doctor what was going on. They were told to stabilize me as quickly as possible and get me to the emergency room in Windsor. I remember the nurses being so apologetic about not wanting to hurt me as they stuck IV needles in both arms. By the time they were done, I had six IV lines in me. The ride to

Windsor took forty-five minutes. The doctor decided to ride along to make sure I remained stable. I remember people talking to me, but I wasn't sure what they or I was saying.

By the time I got to Windsor they had me fairly stable with an increase in blood pressure, but I still had the fever. I was rushed to the intensive care room. I was assigned a nurse, and they quickly moved me into a bed and started to work on me. The doctors knew I had an infection, but they didn't know what type it was. When that happens, they start antibiotics and hope it will take effect. The next twenty-four hours were critical. I was falling asleep and waking up. It seemed every time I would wake up there would be someone new there. My wife had to drive to Windsor by herself, which must have been horrible for her to not know how I was doing and then to try to find me. My sister was notified and came to Windsor from Paris, Ontario, which is about three hours away. Darren was there, but I don't remember much of the first three days. I don't know if it was the infection that caused me to be drowsy, or if the hospital was medicating me to keep me quiet.

This infection was very serious, and my life was in danger. They treated me for common types of infections, but it would take forty-eight hours until the type would be known and they could give me the proper treatment. I was in the intensive care unit for three days. I was then put into a private room for another seven days. They informed me I had gone into septic shock. We learned a great deal from that episode. My sides were hurting, and I had a large bruise where I had fallen.

My wife and I were grateful for the help she had received. Mac had been walked and taken care of by our neighbors, the Wilkinsons. We learned that our true friends would help my wife with the chores if needed, and they came over at all hours just to check up on me. We learned later how important these friends would really become.

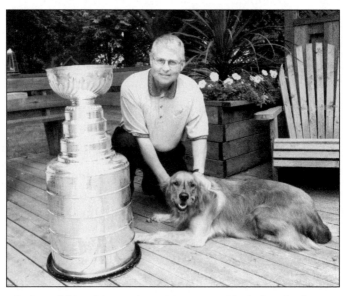

Craig and his golden retriever, Mac, pose with the Stanley Cup.

A Call for Help

This was the first training camp
that I missed.
To a Canadian father,
the sound of blades on the ice
in the fall
is a sound of beauty.
It would be months until I saw
a live game and enjoyed
my fall tradition
of the past eighteen years.

I received a call from Darren one morning. He sounded terrible, and I was upset. I decided to let him talk while I listened. He said he had screwed up and was in trouble. The trouble he had was with alcohol and his ability to handle it. I knew it was not a time for me to lecture. He said he would call back later when he felt he could talk longer. It was a long two days until he called again.

As he talked to me, I could hear the concern in his voice. I told him we each had a problem that we couldn't do much about. We both had to learn to live with our problems. I asked him if he would be upset if I had not gone to the doctor about my cancer. He said that it would be crazy not to treat it. I told him that he had a disease, too, and asked him what he was going to do about it. He agreed he had a problem, and he agreed to get some help. We made a pact that, no matter what happened, we would go through our diseases together and help each other when needed.

Darren informed me he would go into treatment. One of the things I am most proud of was his willingness to go the Red Wing management and tell them he had a problem. He went in with a plan and was not looking for their pity. He did what a responsible person would do and set his priorities and stuck to them. I was concerned the story would get out and that Darren would be put under pressure from the fans. He knew he could never drink again.

His life as a hockey player avails him of many privileges that normal people don't have. He gets paid a lot of money, and has people fawning over him. Many times when he is out to eat, someone will send over a drink. Darren would have to learn to look the other way and deal with those pressures. Now when someone offers to buy him a drink, he will accept, but only if it's a Coke.

The problem of being an alcoholic is compounded by the places and people you are around. True friends understood the problem and decided to not drink when around Darren. July 8, 1996, was a good day. We both agreed to help each other through our diseases. I felt that we had finally communicated as a father and son should. I learned to respect his judgement and his will to succeed. His passion for wanting to win was back in his own life.

The next few months would prove to be a challenge for both of us. I was scheduled to go to Toronto in July for my transplant, and Darren was going to treatment.

Preparing for the Transplant

We made our trip to Toronto and started the process for the transplant. There are several procedures required to harvest the stem cells. I had to have another line put into my chest like the first one I had. I was nervous about it but went ahead and had it done. They give you a local anesthetic, and then you walk to an operating table. Because the hospital was a teaching one, some of the procedures are done by what I will call rookies. They are doctors who are specializing and need to practice. A doctor placed the line in me, and it seemed to go fairly well. The procedure is to then get an X-ray to see if it is located properly. I had the X-ray and was rushed back into the operating room. The line was too short, and a new one would have to be installed. Unfortunately, the anesthetic was wearing off as they did the surgery. It did hurt, but I got through it.

The next procedure is to harvest the stem cells. In order to make them multiply, I had to take Neuprogen, which is a human growth hormone. We were prepared for the bill from the pharmacy because the doctor had warned us about the cost. My wife would have to pay for it, and our insurance company would reimburse us. Roberta had received a new credit card with a $5,000 limit. The man in front of my wife paid a nominal rate for his prescription and walked out. Her bill came to $5,200.00 and thankfully the credit card went through. The man behind her was shocked and pleased he had insurance to pay for his prescription.

The shots are taken each day for ten days, then you go to the hospital for your collection. The collection takes about three hours at a time. The line that had been placed in me was bent in such a way that it wouldn't flow unless I lay with my right arm over my head. The process was slow because of the bend in the tubing. I had to have three sessions before enough of the blood had been separated. Because of the extra sessions, I needed to have more of the growth hormone. The credit card got used again. We had to pay out over $7,000 that month in prescriptions. I am glad we had insurance, and they were usually fast at paying. I don't know how people have a transplant without insurance. The drugs, my lost time at work, and my wife's lost time added up. We decided that she would take a leave of absence until I was well enough to take care of myself. The idea was, with the transplant in August, for her to return to work in October. The people that owned the company told her to come back when it was best for us.

With all the trips to the hospital for testing, we decided to stay in Toronto rather than drive back and forth. Summertime is a great time to live in the downtown section of Toronto. Many movies are filmed there so we got to see some of the on-location shoots. We would walk over to the hospital, which took twenty minutes. After my appointments we would walk around until we were tired and I wanted to go home. If we had walked too far, we would take a cab back. The area we lived in was like a little community. I was glad my wife felt safe there because she would be alone while I was in the hospital.

Darren was going to his meetings and playing golf. His life had turned around, and we were glad he had made a change in his life. I have learned that change will only take place if a person decides to change. I respected Darren for the strength he was showing, and I hoped it would work out for him.

Because the tube in my body was not in a proper position, the doctors decided to remove it. This was done on an outpatient basis with the doctor removing the stitches, which hold it in place, then pulling it out. The young doctor to do this was from New Zealand, and he was doing a stint in the transplant section. He removed the tube and put his finger with a piece of gauze over the small hole. The last time I had it done it took maybe five minutes for the bleeding to stop, then they put a bandage over the hole and away I went. This time it wouldn't stop bleeding.

He had to keep pressure on it for almost two hours, and finally they gave me a medication to enhance the clotting of the opening. It was a long wait, but I will say we had a nice visit. I was always impressed with the dedication of the young doctors. Their lives revolve around medicine and they live it all day every day. Some had left home and traveled to Toronto to get a specialty with the intention of going back to their native lands to help people. It takes a special person to make the commitment to do what they do.

Commitment was something I had not always followed. I felt you did things because they were there to be done. The truly committed person does what is required to get the job done and has the ability to not let other tasks interfere at the job. I admire people who do more than talk about something. The nurses and doctors I dealt with were as fine a group of people as I have ever met.

Patience

The job of being patient was mine, and Roberta helped me with it. We saw people getting upset about waiting and taking it out on the nurse or the doctor. We decided that we wouldn't ask for a nurse or doctor to rush for us and we wouldn't be upset if they ran behind. We always took a lot of material to read and made the best of the time to visit with each other and talk to others in the waiting rooms. I find people are nervous about going to the doctor. They don't always get doctors who understand their plight. I find that doctors who have been through a major illness themselves or have had disease strike their families understand there is more than just the physical side of being sick.

I won't say all the appointments went smoothly. Many of them took a long time. I had X-rays, ultra-sounds, heart function tests, and breathing and dental tests. I had two or three appointments a week for a period of three weeks. By late July my transplant had been moved for the third time. There are only a certain number of beds to use for transplants and each patient takes a different length of time to recover. Again, we decided to wait patiently and not get upset. I didn't want them rushing me out of the hospital to make room for someone else.

We filled the days with walking around, reading, and becoming a much closer couple. Roberta had the ability to calm me on days when things were not going well, and she helped me stay focused. Being ill with a major disease like cancer is a full-time job. It weighs heavily on your mind, and it can control your life. We decided we would learn to live with it and not let it take control of our lives. I told my wife to plan a trip back to Arizona for the next spring. I felt I would be well enough to travel, and we had decided we wanted to go back to the place where we had made our agreement to go through the rest of our lives together no matter what the outcome.

Roberta is a quiet person who doesn't say much. You never know what she is thinking or how she will handle something. She worries that she will say something she will regret later and believes if she doesn't say anything everything will be okay. I am the opposite. I tend to talk first, and then think and apologize later. This made for some interesting conversations between us. The true test of our relationship was learning to accept the differences we had and not allow a difference of opinion to come between us. I had a newfound respect for her when I heard her talking to the doctors if there was something she didn't understand. I hope that others will find the same peace of heart that we have.

Another Delay

Over the next few weeks I noticed a lump under my right armpit. It was steadily getting bigger. I had a great deal of discomfort when I moved my arm. The doctors were not sure what was causing it. I had been warned that a fever for a person going through cancer treatment is dangerous. After the last trip to the emergency room, I invested in a pocket thermometer that we would carry around with us. One night I started to run a fever. We tracked the rise in temperature. When it hit 101 degrees Fahrenheit we decided to head to the emergency room. It was now about 8:30 at night, and the emergency room of a downtown hospital can be a pretty scary place.

During their first trip to Sedona, Arizona, Craig and Roberta vowed to support each other through the difficult times to come.

I met with a couple of doctors who decided I needed some bloodwork done and an ultrasound of the lump. I was worried about another infection, and I wanted to avoid any more time in the hospital. I can still picture the surgical team having an argument in the hall with a tiny hematologist. They wanted to operate because there was a blood clot in my shoulder causing the pain and the lump was infected. She felt there was no need to rush into the operating room. I am glad she stuck to her guns because they never did operate. I stayed in the hospital and they started another IV to administer the antibiotic. Roberta left around 2:30 AM after I was placed in a room.

I spent the next ten days in the hospital while they were giving me an antibiotic and blood thinners. I was placed on rat poison (coumadin) to try to dissolve the blood clot. I had not become accustomed to staying in the hospital, but we soon had a routine worked out. I admire my wife's ability to manage things while I was not able to. We were finding that the disease was not as bad as the cure. The cure would only give me some time, if I were physically strong enough to take the treatment.

The transplant was postponed until after I was taken off the blood thinner medication. The problem was that I was in remission and waiting could cause it to flare up. The doctors decided to wait a month and then test me to see how I was doing. I felt the best I had in quite some time so we decided to go home. It was now the first of September and Melissa needed to get ready for school. During the time I had been in Toronto, from the middle of July until now, she had stayed with friends and relatives. She is a good kid and we are very proud of her maturity level. At sixteen she was able to function by herself and was not swayed by her peers. She is her own person and very much like her brother in her stubbornness.

A Trip Home

The time spent at home was great. Neighbors had maintained our gardens and the yard looked fantastic. We had the chance to see some friends and my wife's relatives. The three weeks at home made me feel like life was treating me right. The hospital called and asked me to be back for the last week of September. We agreed to do the transplant even though I was on blood thinners. The doctors were concerned that I would bleed internally if the transplant was done. My immune system was gone, and I wouldn't have any way of stopping the bleeding or an infection. The choice was up to me. I felt the danger of the cancer reappearing was greater the longer we waited. I knew the risk had been greatly increased, but we decided to take the chance. I would report to the hospital on October 1, my birthday.

Training camp had started for the Red Wings. This was the first training camp that I missed. To a Canadian father, the sound of blades on the ice in the fall is a sound of beauty. It would be months until I saw a live game and enjoyed my fall tradition of the past eighteen years. There is a series of odors, sights, and thought processes that take place when you go to a game or practice. I was now beginning to understand that what is important in life is not money. It is friends, family, and the love of a good person to travel this journey we are on. I was learning to do what was important and not let the other things get in the way of what I truly wanted.

The Transplant

*I know it sounds simplistic,
but the disease has helped me
become a better person.
It is much better to be grateful
for what you have
than to be upset
about what you don't have.*

The next few weeks taught me what it meant to be a patient. I learned what people who have had a major illness go through. There were days when I didn't feel like going on, but I knew I couldn't give up.

I was admitted on a Sunday with the treatment to start on Monday. I had been poked, prodded, and stuck enough times over the past months that all I wanted was to get this going. The procedure called for two days of intense chemotherapy and then three days of full-body radiation. The chemotherapy went well, but I was losing my desire to eat. The thought of food nauseated me. I would get sick to my stomach when they brought the food to my room. This process was to continue for a long time. I was hooked up to an IV through another shunt in my chest. They explained I would be able to last without the food, because the fluids they were giving me would keep me going.

Full-Body Radiation

The radiation would take place twice a day for a period of three days. I would be taken to the radiation department in a wheelchair. There I would lie on a piece of plywood six inches off the floor. The technicians would then place a ballast on me to even out the effects of the radiation. Because the radiation will travel through the body at an uneven rate, it may overradiate the thinner parts of your body unless a ballast is used.

I was to receive three minutes of radiation per side, twice a day. Every time I went to the radiation department there was a little girl getting her radiation after me. She was going through radiation for a transplant for leukemia. I felt so sorry for her. She never had a smile or looked at the others around her. She wore some great hats to cover the bald head she had from the chemotherapy. I decided to not complain about my troubles. If this little girl could undergo the trials of a transplant, then I would be able to without much problem.

I find that people complain sometimes when they have no reason to. Some people complain when they have lived a full life with food, lodging, family, and friends. I know it sounds simplistic, but the disease has helped me become a better person. I hope others will have this approach to their disease. It is much better to be grateful for what you have than to be upset about what you don't have.

Radiation is like going outside and getting the worst sunburn possible. I hurt in spots that I didn't even know I had. Every person is different in their recovery, so you can't judge one to another. Still, the thought of that little girl going through her radiation gave me strength to make the days more pleasant. The healing process for a person who has gone through radiation is long. It seems like you are sick for a couple of months. One of the other patients told me to think of it as being placed in a microwave, but you continue to cook for a couple of months later.

Stem Cell Rescue

The last day of the radiation is also the day you get your stem cells back. This is called a stem cell rescue. You have no white cell count, and the smallest infection would kill you. Ideally, the new stem cells will start to make white cells and help your immune system recover. There is a danger of infection and the possible rejection of the stem cells by your body. We hoped that the stem cells I received would be clear of the cancer cells, and the use of the cell separator would help. It is still too early to decide if the gamble has paid of.

There is a great deal of pain involved with the radiation. To combat the pain, you are given a morphine drip. I do not like pills of any sort, and the thought of morphine was heavy on my mind. Although it makes the pain bearable, I was concerned that the drug would become a crutch that I would depend on. I asked them to give me half of what they normally would. It became apparent to me the sooner I was off the drugs the faster I would get better.

My wife relays stories about the delusions I had while under the medication. At one point, I thought my dog was smoking a cigar in bed with me, and apparently I became quite upset that my wife wouldn't look in the bed. I also was sure the Blue Angels were flying across the road from the hospital. We would laugh about it later, but at the time it appeared real to me. I saw how dangerous drugs could become. There were times when the cravings for the drug would make me call down to the desk and have the nurses see if they could increase the doses. I am glad my wife was there and understood my wishes. After five days I requested the morphine be stopped. They gradually slowed down the dosage until it was done. I could understand addiction, and I hoped that Darren would be able to handle the challenges he was facing.

Going Home

I was in the hospital for twenty-one days, and then one Saturday morning the doctors came into the room and announced I could go home. I called Roberta and asked her to come immediately. I knew I would feel better at home—the hospital was getting to me. She asked what I would need for clothing, and I said all I needed was a belt and shoes. She took a cab over to the hospital and came into the room. I started to get dressed when I realized the pants I had were actually pajama bottoms. I wasn't going home in pajama bottoms. When Roberta came into the room, I was sitting on the edge of the bed. I explained my problem, and she went back to the apartment to retrieve a pair of pants. She had the cab driver wait until she had gone up to the apartment, then take her back to the hospital.

The excitement of leaving was soon balanced by the reality of trying to resume life after the hospital visit. I was taken to the entrance in a wheelchair. When the cab came to pick me up, I was so weak I couldn't lift my leg to get into the cab. I turned around and sat down, then Roberta lifted my legs up and helped me in the cab. When I got to the apartment, the process had to be reversed. It was a major amount of work to lift my leg up to get over the curb. By the time I was in the elevator I was winded and getting dizzy. Roberta helped me to the apartment and into bed. It was the middle of the afternoon, and I slept until after 7:00 the next morning.

The morning started with me being sick to my stomach. I was trying to eat, something I had not done for a while. People called to wish us well, but I was not in the mood to talk to anyone. I felt like I had gone ten rounds with a boxer and had been on the receiving end of a lot of punches. I was more tired than I can describe. It was a major accomplishment to walk in a circle around the apartment: through the dining room, the kitchen, and the living room. It was a small, one bedroom apartment and I am sure there was only twenty-five to thirty feet of walking to make this trip but it seemed like forever.

I was looking forward to eating again, but my stomach wouldn't allow much. I got sick every time I ate and I joked that I would only rent the food for a short while. One of the nurses in the hospital was of Russian heritage. She and I became acquainted during my stay. When she worked the room for the first time, I asked what part of Russia she was from. She was surprised that I knew she was from Russia. She said most people never make the connection. I informed her that my son played hockey with many Russians and their dialect was the same as hers. She told me when I went home to drink the broth made from chickens. She told my wife to add water, chicken parts, and an onion and boil it. I drank this for the better part of a week. This definitely helped me learn to eat again. The radiation causes the lining of the stomach and the intestinal tract to be irritated, which is why I got sick when I ate. It would take time.

I left the hospital at 240 pounds, the same weight I had gone in at. I ballooned with the steroids, and

Darren, Cheryl, and Griffin.

now I wasn't getting the IV bags to keep my weight up. In the next three weeks I lost over forty pounds. I ate a part of a banana for breakfast, a piece of toast for lunch, and usually some broth for dinner. Just the thought of eating made me sick.

We felt it would be best if I stayed in Toronto for a couple of weeks until I was strong enough to travel home. During this time I had appointments at the hospital. These trips were all-day events. By the time I got up, dressed, and got back, it took a lot out of me. I was concerned that I wouldn't get better. The improvement in one week was minimal. I worked at walking in the apartment, and finally we went for a walk in the street in front of the apartment. I was out of breath by the time we hit the sidewalk. We took a short walk and went back upstairs. This would be all the exercise I got while we lived in Toronto.

Year Four, 1996-97

The hockey season had started. Training camp was over, and the regular season was underway. It was now November and I had not seen Darren, Cheryl, and Griffin since September. The Red Wings were in town to play the Maple Leafs. I knew I would not be allowed to go to the game, but I did get to go to the hotel to see Darren. It was good to give him a hug, and I fought back the tears. I was proud of his accomplishments and most proud of the decision he made the summer before. He gives me strength through his ability to adapt to any situation. I realize he is only human, but I also appreciate what he went through to get to where he is.

It would be the end of December before I would be allowed to go to a game in person. At home we had a satellite dish, so at least I got to watch all the games. My strength improved at a slow pace. There were times when I didn't feel any progress was being made, but my wife reminded me of the steps I could now do. She returned to work in January, and I was left to fend for myself. The two months previous, we had friends who would come over to babysit me if Roberta had to leave for a while. It took my wife some time to feel confident in my ability to stay by myself.

I was still getting sick, but I had bottomed out on the weight loss. I was now at 185 pounds. If only I would stay there. I had no desire to eat, and food still caused me to be sick. It is tough to eat when you know it will make you sick. I was getting better because I was sick only a couple of times a day—not at every meal. Roberta worked hard to make sure I ate, and I know she was upset when I would get sick. Over the next months, I gradually got to the point where I wouldn't get sick at all. What a relief to eat a meal and keep it down.

The Red Wings were doing well, with the Stanley Cup as their goal. Darren was having a good year until the middle of January when he dislodged a bone in his right hand. It caused the circulation to be cut off to his fingers. It was serious enough that he spent the All-Star break in the hospital getting treatment. I made my first drive to see him and got my butt whipped playing cards. It was good to see him doing well and know he had his life in control. There was a calm about him that I had not seen before.

Darren went on to have the best season yet. Many of the reporters were quick to ask if his decision to not drink had made him a better hockey player. Darren would respond that he wasn't sure, but it didn't hurt. The team was poised to make a run for the cup.

A month after Craig's transplant, he and Roberta were able to visit with Darren before a game.

The Cup

*Tears came to my eyes
as I realized I was alive
to witness my son
realizing a dream.*

I won't go into each game and every series because that is in the record books. I will say that the men Darren was playing with had a goal. They had been to the finals two years ago and got beat out by Colorado the next year. They went through adversity and came back with a single goal in mind: to win the Stanley Cup. Colorado made the Red Wings a better team because they taught them how to lose with dignity. There was an ugly incident with Kris Draper being hit from behind by Claude Lemieux. Kris needed surgery to repair a broken jaw. Claude laughed about it and said he had made Kris famous. I knew there was bad blood between the teams, and I knew a hockey player would always avenge a wrong. Kris was one of Darren's best friends, so I also knew that Darren would stick up for him.

Sweet Revenge

March 26, 1997, was the final game against Colorado, and the teams were playing each other very tightly. There had been no attempt to even the score by the Red Wings until this night. The teams had played six times between the incident last year and March 26.

During the first period Igor Larionov was being worked over by Peter Forsberg. The rest of the players squared off, and Darren looked Lemieux in the eye and went at him swinging. Lemieux went into a turtle position and covered his head. Darren pulled him over to the Red Wing bench and gave him a good licking.

The referee broke the fights up and dispatched people to the penalty box. Darren received four minutes for roughing but was left in the game. It makes you wonder why the referee didn't kick him out for being in the second group to fight after the stoppage of play. The team went on to tie the score, and then Darren scored the game-winning goal in overtime. Justice was almost complete. The next step was to go on to win the Stanley Cup. The team went into the playoffs with the attitude that you have to maintain composure. It takes sixteen winning games to clench the oldest prize in team sports, and they knew what to do. The team didn't get too high after a win or too down on themselves when they lost. They maintained their focus and put their trust in the coaches and each other.

Victory at Last

For those who didn't get a chance to see the final game against Philadelphia, Darren scored a great goal. He made moves that only talented hockey players can make. That goal will be shown on highlight shows for years to

Darren's fight with Claude Lemieux during the final game with the Avalanche in 1997 avenged the hit Red Wing Kris Draper received from Lemieux the previous year.

come. Not known for his skating, Darren was now turning into a finesse player. I was in awe of the goal from the stands, but I really appreciated it more when I viewed it on television. What a difference a year can make.

The celebration after the game was incredible. Tears came to my eyes as I realized I was alive to witness my son realizing a dream. Every Canadian boy plays each game with the Stanley Cup as the final goal. Very few ever get the opportunity to play for it. The Red Wings were led by Steve Yzerman, who led by example. I know that sounds corny, but many people try to lead by telling people what to do. A good example is the proper way to lead. The team was in the throes of excitement. There were hundreds of people in a dressing room usually reserved for the players and coaches. Unfortunately some of the people in the dressing room should not have been allowed in. I talked later to some of the press who said their credentials had been ripped from their necks. Strangers were walking out of the dressing room with souvenirs and many of the items meant for the players. It was too hot in the dressing room so I left and stood in the hall.

I was in the same spot in the hall where Don Cherry and I had a conversation earlier regarding his wife Rose. For those who are unfamiliar with Don, he is the ultimate Canadian hockey fan. Don grew up as a career minor league player who played but one game in the

Father and son in the Red Wings' locker room.

NHL. He is a fan of the lunch bucket player like Darren. It is considered an honor to be included in one of Don's videos about hockey and Darren has been included in a couple of them.

Don's wife Rose was going through a transplant similar to mine because of another type of cancer. I had approached Don to see if he would help me get the message to the public about the type of cancer I had. He opened up to me that his wife was undergoing a transplant and things were not going well. Unfortunately, she did not make it. I felt so sorry for Don's loss. She was everything to him. They were a team. Rose always let Don be Don.

I was overcome with emotion and vowed to help raise money for cancer research. I couldn't bear another conversation with someone who had lost a family member. The evening was just beginning. The players posed with the Cup and family and friends. We sat around the locker room not wanting to leave until all the sights and sounds could be taken in. Grown men cried with emotion and played like little kids. The press was always looking for one more player to interview. I was full of adrenaline and not at all tired. The party then went to a restaurant north of the city.

It was 2:30 AM and there were still fans in the streets. We drove to the restaurant, and Darren and I went into the bar and watched the replay of his goal. The rest of the team was still celebrating when Darren took his turn to drink from the cup. The traditional drink is champagne or beer. Darren poured the existing liquor out onto the carpet and poured in a soft drink. I then knew he was going to be able to take care of his family. This made me the proudest parent in the room. The chance for him to be swayed was there, and he chose to stay on course. I also remembered that there was a team who lost that night. I hope these players' parents helped them get through the pain of losing. If they were to succeed, they would have to learn how to lose as a team before they could win as a team, just as the Red Wings had.

Darren shares the Stanley Cup with Craig and his "old-timer" team, the Blues.

Tragedy Strikes

On the Friday night after the Stanley Cup win, the lives of the Red Wings would change forever. Two of the players and the team masseuse were in a limousine after a day of golfing with the team. Darren called our house at 11:00 PM and told me there had been an accident with some of the players. He wanted to call his house and tell his wife before she heard it from someone else.

Just as I hung the phone up the television flashed the news. The limo driver ran off the road, causing the vehicle to run into a tree. Injured where Slava Fetisov, Vladimir Konstantinov, and Sergei Mnatsakanov. Slava would play again the next year, but the careers of

Vladimir Konstantinov and Sergei Mnatsakanov were over. With months of recovery ahead of them, the normal challenges of everyday life became barriers. They had to learn how to eat and perform even the smallest task. Life does throw us curves every once in a while. It was sad seeing a great warrior like Vladimir sitting in a wheelchair. I felt sorry for Vladi and Sergei's families, who would have to struggle with a great deal over the years to come. I admire their wives for showing the strength their husbands couldn't.

We always remember them in our prayers and admire the courage with which they work each day. I saw the team together a few days later on the television. These grown men who were heroes only a week before were moved to tears. I will always remember these men, and I am sure the players will never forget the contributions they made to the team. I believe it gave the team strength, which they would harness for the upcoming season.

Year Five, 1997-98

Playing hockey until the end of June, celebrating the Cup win, and dealing with the terrible accident had made the summer go by quickly. Before we knew it the players were trying to get back into shape for training camp. Some of them said the summer was so short they hadn't lost their game conditioning.

With the season just around the corner, it was decided that the team would go to Northern Michigan for training camp. Scotty Bowman felt the team needed to be in a place where they could bond and get back to the close-knit group they had been the year before. It was going to be difficult for the team since two valued members, Sergei and Vladi, were on the mend but would never be more than bystanders to the game. Vladi's locker in the dressing room had changed little from the last game of the Stanley Cup series the previous spring. It looked like he could come through the door and suit up at any given moment.

The team played the season with mixed emotions; it seemed that in some games they were just going through the motions. Sergei Fedorov was in a contract dispute with the management. He was missed for his ability to change the flow of a game by doing what he did best—score. I was impressed with Steve Yzerman who rarely had a bad game. He was the ultimate competitor and started the season where he had left off. Steve would block shots, play on the power play, and kill penalties, and it appeared he had a renewed spring in his skating. The Stanley Cup win seemed to have taken ten years off Steve's age.

The players knew it didn't matter where they ended the regular season, but where they ended up after the playoffs. They seemed to be focusing on the playoffs and used the inspiration of Vladi and Sergei as a catalyst for the season. At the end of the year the playoffs started with the first round against Phoenix. They proved to be a tough team and it took six games to move on to the next series against St. Louis, which also went six games. They then moved on to play Dallas, the team to beat in the West. Dallas had the best record of the year and looked like they would make Detroit a victim of their offense. The Red Wings played hard and eliminated the Stars in another hard-fought, six-game series.

The playoffs are a tough time of the year for the players because they are away from their families for the better part of the two months it takes to play the postseason. The 1997-98 season had been especially hard on the players because the NHL had compressed the schedule to make time to play in the Olympics. Now the teams were showing the stress of a long season and a hard-fought playoff. Each game in the playoffs was like a battle.

The next series in the playoffs was against Washington. They had succeeded in winning the Eastern division and would contest the Red Wings for the Stanley Cup. The Red Wings were focused and understood the commitment needed to make a run for the cup. Washington was ready for Detroit but I think they underestimated the Wings and their desire to win.

The games were played for Vladi and Sergei, who were at the arena for Game Four of the Dallas series. Detroit won the first two games against Washington at home and flew to Washington to make the sweep complete.

Our family made arrangements to fly to Washington the afternoon of Game Four. Detroit had won Game Three and we wanted to be there for the final game. We had a flight from Detroit to Washington arranged for 5:00 PM that would arrive in time for us to check into a hotel and go to the game. We got on the plane, taxied out from the gate, and then ended up parked on the runway. There was a storm on the East Coast which was severe enough to stop air traffic from coming into the Washington area. We sat on the plane for three hours and finally got back to the gate in time to unload and watch the puck drop in Washington on a TV in the airport bar.

We were disappointed about not getting to the game but we put it in perspective. There was no one hurt and no harm done. We went home and watched the end of the game at our house. Darren was asking where his parents were because he knew we were going to the game. The next day we had a chance to see him and the team and enjoy the thrill of the win. I will always remember seeing Steve hand the Cup to Vladi in his wheelchair while the rest of the team crowded around. It was a fitting end to the season.

179

Darren proudly holds Stanley over his head after the Red Wings' second Cup win.

The Foundation

*We help patients
learn to become advocates
for themselves.*

The day before Father's Day in June of 1997 Darren called me. He told me a lawyer would be giving me a call and to answer the questions to the best of my ability. I was a little surprised and asked Darren what was going on. He told me we were going to start a foundation to help people with my disease and to raise money for research. I got the call from the lawyer, and the McCarty Cancer Foundation was started. On Father's Day, Darren and I talked about what we could do to help others.

Darren felt that with his popularity in the Detroit market, he could help me get exposure. He would have very little time to work with the Foundation, but I could help. We felt it would be good to get some publicity about the disease multiple myeloma. Darren felt we could help others with the disease if we could show people that cancer is a disease that may not be beaten but can be lived with. News of the foundation was sent to the press. One of the fundraising ideas was a limited edition print signed by the 1996-1997 Stanley Cup team. We had only ninety-seven of these prints (for the '97 season), and unfortunately, this was the last thing that Vladimir Konstantinov signed before his accident. We had them framed, and presented one to each of the players. Each player received his team number of the signed print as a way of showing our appreciation for doing the signing. Mr. Ilitch and Scotty Bowman also received copies of the print. We used the money from the remaining prints to fund support groups and research.

The Foundation was to be funded through the sale of clothing at the local Meijer stores. Darren had a line of clothing through a marketing firm owned by Jeff Beckett. Jeff cut a deal with Meijer to have five percent of the sales put back into the Foundation. The first check was presented to us at a press conference we had on October 28, 1998. The check was for $45,000.

Reaching Out

I have found that the best method of hope is to see someone who is living with the same disease. I admire people like Myron Wahls who deal with multiple myeloma on a daily basis and show others that life does go on. Myron is a judge in the Detroit area who has multiple myeloma and has succeeded in trying to live a normal life. He is a fantastic pianist who has toured with some of the world's jazz legends. He gives me strength when I see him perform as a pianist and do his job as a judge. I admire him as a role model of how to live with a fatal disease and not let it take control of your life.

Unfortunately, we must also remember those who succumb to the disease. I was not accustomed to talking with sick or dying people. I was always afraid I would say the wrong thing. I have learned over the past year that sometimes it is best to say nothing. The best thing you can do is listen and be a sounding board for the person who is sick.

I have had many people call and talk to me. I feel fortunate to have at my disposal many fine patients with my disease who will talk to newly diagnosed patients. We help patients learn to become advocates for themselves. We have also educated a few doctors along the way. I hope we are helping people overcome their fears. I admire Darren and what he has done because he is living every day with a disease just as I am. We fear the unknown, and similar to AA, we wish to give support to those afflicted with multiple myeloma.

The Foundation has received many contributions. Some of these contributions came from fundraising events in which people sold raffle tickets. There were donations made from fun runs, penny drives, bowling marathons, and corporations. One of the best fundraisers we had was with a hockey mothers' organization where we raised $20,000, and through a sharing of the money, they received $6,000 back into their system. They used the money for a banquet for their players.

Ulterior Motives

We turn away most requests for fundraisers because the people usually have other motives to help. Many times they want Darren to make an appearance in conjunction with a store opening before they will make a donation. This may sound like a little work for a lot of money but Darren's time is valuable in that he needs to spend it with his family. Most fans think playing hockey is not a full-time job. I know it looks glamorous to travel all over the country, but the travel is long and the nights are short. Most of the fellows go out to get something to eat after the game then they try to get some sleep. It may be 2:00 am before they get to bed. If they have small kids, they get up with them in the morning and then travel to the rink for practice. Practice is held every day from the first day of training camp until the end of the year. The routine changes very little from team to team. The Red Wings are owned by the Ilitch family, who understand the stress of playing professional sports. To keep the team from being worn down by travel, they bought them a plane. When a game is over, they often fly straight home. A trip to the West Coast would add a couple of extra days of travel were it not for the plane.

The coaching staff works hard to make sure the players are fresh and not overworked. I know the team performs better because the management realizes the importance of team play. Again, they lead by example.

Support Group

I was happy running the Foundation with my wife and a couple of friends. We thought we could do a pretty good job if we had a couple of fundraisers and started a support group. The support group was started after I had a meeting at our house with four other families affected by multiple myeloma. These people were the first of many we would contact. Over the next six months we started support groups in Windsor, Detroit, and Toronto. The groups usually consist of twenty-five people, most of whom have the disease. They meet every two months for a couple of hours. A guest speaker may give some helpful information, or it may be a session where people ask questions among themselves. We don't give any medical advice, but we do have people in the group who have had treatment in almost every area of medicine that relates to our disease.

The groups also allow the caregivers the opportunity to talk with each other. They need as much attention as the patients because they are the ones who have to keep us going. They are the ones who give us hope even when they may feel it is hopeless. I admire the caregivers and their dedication to us. Many members of the group are caregivers who have lost a spouse and continue to come to the meetings. We are like a family. I tell patients that the Foundation is a group of people ready to help them on a journey so they won't have to go alone. It must be frightening to be by yourself when you are sick. We can't give people unrealistic perceptions about their health, but we can assure them we will support them even if they decide to do nothing as far as treatment.

Sometimes the treatment scares people. Cancer is a word that will send most people into a depression. I have been fortunate to talk to many fine individuals who have the strength to carry on, in spite of cancer or other diseases. They truly give me inspiration. I feel lucky to have met these wonderful people and I enjoy meeting their families and friends. When I feel a little down, I remember some of these people and I recover from the blues quickly. Most of these people are sick, but they want to help someone else. It reminds me of my grandfather, who when he was eighty, would go down to help the old folks in the nursing home. I guess your attitude has a lot to do with how you feel.

I won't say every day is Pollyanna-ish, but life isn't bad. I am sure the problems I have are minor compared to others, and I hope to help people realize how fortunate they are even if their health is not that good. We should be thankful that we live where we do, and that we have the resources available to us so we do not worry about what we don't have. When you become sick, there is a lot of time to think about your values and the goals you want to attain. As Darren would say, you need to set your priorities.

Room for Growth

When the Foundation was but a couple of months old, Darren arranged for me to meet a friend of his, John Matouk. John is in his early thirties and very success-ful. He wanted to help the Foundation and arranged a "Stanley Cup" party at a local golf club. Through his efforts, we raised over $30,000 from that event.

One day John sat down with me and asked me what my goals were. I told him that I wanted to help peo-ple with cancer. He knew I had been in business for twenty-five years so he asked me to consider running the Foundation like a business.

With John's help, we found Pat Kelly. Pat is the advertising manager for the *Wall Street Journal* and he agreed to assist me with the Foundation. John then gave us an office in his building to use. Patty Vincent became our first paid employee. With an MBA, she was overqualified, and I know she is grossly underpaid.

When she took the job, I was impressed with how compassionate she is. She can talk to someone and make that person feel good even when things may not be going well. Her approach to work is refreshing. There is no task she won't do, and I feel she understands my goals. Both Pat and Patty are people who understand what it is like to be sick and give of themselves, with all the time they have.

Showing Off the Cup

The summer of 1997 was filled with talk of the Stanley Cup and when Darren would bring it into our town. The Leamington area is home to H. J. Heinz and a tomato festival is held there annually in August. I had many people call and ask if Darren would bring the Cup home for the parade. The team decides who gets the Cup and when. Being the team they are, they took turns by drawing names out of a hat. Darren's turn was in September, but we couldn't convince people of that. We heard many stories about the Cup coming to the Tomato Festival Parade and how the town didn't want a crowd problem so they hadn't announced it officially. In reality, the Cup was in Russia that weekend, but we couldn't convince everyone that that was the truth. Many people called our house and asked what time the Cup would arrive and where they should stand to get the best view. I even went on the local radio to

The McCarty family with the Stanley Cup.

explain that the Cup would not be there for the parade, yet people were still convinced of the opposite.

We made arrangements to have the Cup brought to Leamington on September 2 with Darren available for a private showing for the first hour and a half. We made an announcement in the local paper and on local radio that the public would have an opportunity to see the cup from 7:00 until 10:00 PM. Darren would not stay for pictures. I admire Darren for wanting to do the right thing when it came to the public. He would rather meet and talk to twenty-five kids than sit at a table and sign autographs for an hour. He wanted to be able to relate to the kids and enjoy their company. You can't do that if you are in a production line signing autographs. I took a lot of grief over him not wanting to appear when the general public would have the opportunity to see the Cup. It was agreed he would skate around the arena with the Cup and then say a few words to the crowd.

The family had a reception at Darren's grandmother's house with aunts, uncles, neighbors, and friends invited. About 150 people made their way out to see Stanley. The Cup has a mystique about it and when Darren first set it down at his grandmother's, most people were too shy to come close. After a couple of minutes the crowd became comfortable enough to move in

Griffin McCarty, age 1, with the Stanley Cup.

for pictures. After the reception Darren took the Cup to his grandfather's grave. I know Bob was proud of Darren. He then took the Cup to the Leamington Arena.

The evening went great, with over four hundred people coming through to get their picture taken with Darren. This was a private function for the people Darren felt had helped him get to the NHL. It was full of old coaches, old teammates, friends, teachers, and their families. It was refreshing to see Darren remember most of the people by name and visit with them.

At 7:00 he skated into the arena with the Cup. There were 1,200 people in the building and the flashes on the cameras where going off everywhere. Chills ran down my spine as Darren did a slow skate around the rink and then set the Cup at center ice while he gave an inspiring talk about following your dreams. He said you have to pay the price if you really want something, but if you work hard you may get the opportunity to have your own Stanley Cup as a reward. Many people have come up to me since his speech and said it has helped their child focus on a goal and work hard to get there.

With the Cup in hand, he made one final skate around the ice and then left to change for dinner with family and friends. The crowd was good until the police locked the doors. Once they had as many people in the building as they felt could see the Cup in the time allowed, they shut the doors. When I got back to the arena at 9:00 PM, there were still four hundred people outside in the rain. The police informed me they wouldn't go home. I felt sorry that these people would not get to see the Cup or Darren, but there is only so much you can do. Thanks to the Red Wings organization and the Ilitch family, we were able to arrange for the Cup to come back to Leamington during a Red Wing alumni game later in the fall. I hope that those who missed the Cup in September got the chance to see it that time.

More Health Problems

My health was not good, and I was concerned. I made a trip to Toronto to visit my doctor, Keith Stewart. He went through a series of tests. Keith called me at the hotel that night and said he thought I had something called Addison's disease. It is a disease of the adrenal gland. He told me that, through medication, I would gain energy and the desire to keep going. This continued until the spring of 1998 when I started to feel bad again. We went to Florida for a vacation in February. I didn't feel well, and I knew something was wrong. When I got back home, I went in and found my blood count was low. I was having trouble keeping platelets, and I felt sluggish. I had a blood transfusion, and it was discovered that my blood pressure was high. I was getting headaches and sick to my stomach. Back into the hospital I went. This trip lasted for ten days. This time I had a problem with my pituitary gland. I had something called Graves' disease.

We were in the middle of organizing a major fundraising dinner and I was not able to help. Darren jumped in and made phone calls to get the word out about the dinner. It was a black-tie affair for six hundred people. Two weeks before the event we had only two hundred people registered, but the event turned out great. I thank Darren, Pat, Patty, Melissa, John Matouk, and Dorothy Martin, the volunteer coordinator, for the evening's success. We raised over $200,000 that night. This would go a long way in research.

A Little Help from Our Friends

I appreciate all the contributions people have made to us. I will acknowledge one person in particular. Every month we receive a check for $2.00 from one woman. I am sure that $2.00 is a great portion of her income, but she continues to send it to us. I will always value the people who contribute to us when I know they are using their hard-earned money to do it. We don't ask people to take money away from other charities, but we do ask them to dig deeper to give to us. I feel responsible for the money, and I will always make sure it is used properly. Too many charities don't use the money for what it is intended. We do have many expenses that have to be paid, but we have been fortunate in having a lot of them covered. One firm, Midnight Oil, has donated all the marketing, the printing of a pamphlet was done by Rusas Printing Company, and a computer, software, and computer help were also donated to us.

There are many fine people who help like Karen Chase of Chase Publications. She developed a print for Darren to sign with the profits coming back to the foundation. We are helping more people, and the money for research will be significant. There are many great people in the world. Many times the good deeds are overshadowed by the bad ones. I hope Darren and I can show you that living with a problem does not mean you have to live your life in total exile.

A Final Word

I hope you get the chance to have your kids impress you the way my son impresses me. I learned to be a better father, husband, and human when I learned to respect people for their differences. I have learned not to judge people by what others say but by how they treat me and my family. I wish I did not have cancer, but I also know cancer may have saved me from becoming a miserable old man. I thank all who have helped Darren and me develop as a father and son. We truly respect each other.

Darren and Craig standing above Joe Louis Arena.

To Darren, last year you gave me a foundation for Father's Day, this year I give you this book. I want you to know what a positive influence you have made on my life and the lives of those around you. I love you and I see you becoming a great father, husband, and person. Hockey may be what has given you the lifestyle you have, but your thoughtfulness will keep you going for years to come.

AFTERWORD

To me this book is really about a dream. Different people have different dreams. Mine was to play in the NHL. But it is also about family and the support needed to achieve. I'm the first to admit that without the love and support of my parents, and their allowing me to become my own person, I may not be who I am today.

My family is no different than any other. We've had our good times and our bad times, but through it all, we've always used those experiences and tried to make them positive.

I am also very proud of my Dad for not only the person he is and the support he has given me, but also that in a time where things could be so bad, he goes out of his way to make sure everyone else, either those with multiple myeloma or their caregivers, is helped.

One thing my Dad always said to me was "Whatever you do, do it to the best of your ability so you can never say 'if I only worked a little harder, I could have done it.'" That advice has always stuck with me. If you want something enough, I believe you can achieve it. It's all about a matter of priorities.

I've always said I never want to work a day in my life and so far it's working out.

Darren McCarty

Craig McCarty was born in Leamington, Ontario, on October 1, 1949. He has lived most of his life in and around the Leamington area. From the mid-seventies until he was diagnosed with cancer, Craig ran his own business. It was a difficult transition from managing his own company to being under the control of doctors and other medical practitioners.

He and his family have averaged over 100 hockey games a year since Darren's career started over twenty years ago. Craig now runs the McCarty Cancer Foundation.